Courtship
In a
Shoebox

by

Nancy Mae McClintock

Sally
Enjoy & God Bless
Nancy

Polar Photography Publishing
www.polarphotography.com
Cover Design by Polar Photography
Cover Image New Martinsville, West Virginia (cir. 1900)

ISBN: 13: 978-17346912-0-7
ISBN: 10: 1-7346912-04

DEDICATION

I dedicate this book to my mother, Gladys Patterson Taylor. Because of her diligence in saving these letters throughout the years, this book has become a reality.

CONTENTS

ACKNOWLEDGMENTS

First and foremost I praise God for answered prayers and
my brother Bill Taylor, who after many phone calls, helped me in
remembering many details. Also, I am grateful to friends and
family for their encouragement and the Florida Writers Association
at Lady Lake for their help in editing. And lastly, I would like to
thank Chris and Eileen Malinger for putting this together.

PREFACE

This is the story of the courtship of Frank Vernon Patterson, born in 1881 and Martha Lillian Covert born in 1882. They were in their early twenties when they started this relationship. Frank lived on the family farm in Butler County in Western Pennsylvania. Martha grew up in Rose Point, a little village along the main highway where she lived in what you will come to know as the "Stone House." It was about five miles from the Patterson farm. Martha moved from Rose Point to New Castle, a bustling city about fifteen miles away, where some of her family lived. But after a while she traveled to West Virginia to live with some other family members.

In January1999, I was cleaning out closets in my mother's home and I found a treasure; there were 155 letters tucked away in an old shoebox. They were from my grandparents, Frank and Martha Patterson, written to one another during their courtship. The letters were dated from 1901 to 1905. I read them during my vacation and they touched my heart. They made me see what a rich heritage I have and I was immersed in a gentler time of history and love. As I read these letters, I found there was much to learn, so I have attempted to investigate and record. I share these letters not to pry into one's past, but for us to receive a blessing over a century later.

It has been many years since I looked at the letters. Our lives were busy with life because family and jobs were the priority. But as time would have it, my own dear husband of 37 years passed away in 2018 so I was able to devote the hours it took to write the history of my grandparents. I believe it is important to record these letters not just for the innocence and graciousness of the time, but to see how dependence on the Lord helped to keep this relationship intact.

INTRODUCTION

In the early 1990's my mother and I were going for a ride and she was showing me old family places and telling me about her family's history. She took me to the Stone House and said, "Pull up in the driveway and let's see if we can go in." She knocked on the door and told the woman who answered that her mother grew up in this house. The lady invited us in. I remember her husband showing us the window sills. He explained that they were eighteen inches deep because that is how thick the stone walls were in this old house. The rooms were small and there had been many additions over the years. A stone house was unusual in the early nineteen hundreds because most houses were made of wood. I felt privileged to have been able to see this Stone House.

The Patterson farm was located about sixty miles from our home in Blawnox, PA. We traveled there almost every holiday and I was able to spend several weeks at the farm during the summer. This beautiful location in Western Pennsylvania has rolling hills and wide open country. The fields of crops were colorful with rows going in different directions, making it look like a patchwork quilt.

There were three houses and two large red barns as well as various out-buildings on the farm. One building behind the large house was a store the century before. On our visits, my brother and I would investigate the buildings. One house was about a hundred yards from the lower barn and we were told my great-grandfather and great-mother, Jesse and Lizzie Patterson, lived there at one time. It was now used as a chicken coop and eventually demolished. I never liked going into this house because I didn't like the smell of the chickens. We found an interesting room that had old antiques and an old telephone on the wall that had a crank to turn that made a bell sound. It wasn't connected to anything but we were fascinated.

The lower barn was for the cows and was adjacent to a large field. This barn was two stories with hay in the top level and cows in the lower floor. We would go to the cow barn and watch as the cows were milked. They had air compressor milkers. It was fun to watch them attach the milkers to the cows' teats and listen to the rhythmic sound of milking six cows at a time. There were always a few kittens in the barn waiting for a squirt of milk. Across from the big double doors of the barn was the milk house. Inside there were ten gallon cans filled with milk and stored in a spring of cold water.

Behind the milk house was a large shed where dried corn was kept. There was an electric corn husking machine and we kids would turn it on and try to use it. We knew that if we got caught, we would be in big trouble. Across from that was a fence where we could see the pigs. I really loved watching them when they were "slopped." They got to eat all the discards our garbage disposals get today.

Down a long pathway was a house where my Aunt Leona, Uncle Cecil, and Cousin Carl lived. We were told that my mother was born there so Grandma and Granddad lived there when they were first married.

Across the road from all these buildings, up on the knoll of the hill, sat the gracious, large, stately main farm house where my grandma and granddad lived. My mother lived in this house growing up. I

3

remember sleeping in her bedroom which was up a long narrow stairway. There were three other bedrooms upstairs and most of them had fireplaces that no longer worked. My grandparent's bedroom was on the first floor. I remember sitting on her bed and watching Grandma look into the mirror of her beautiful marble top dresser. She would make a long braid of hair then wrap it in a bun and use many big bobby pins to fix it on the back of her head. I still use this same dresser in my bedroom because my mother saved it over many years and gave it to me in 1981.

My brother Bill and I would follow granddad around and as he walked with a cane, he would tap me on my leg and say, "Get out of my road." We would follow him into the chicken coop and gather eggs then he would take them to the cave, an actual manmade cave in the ground. It was musty and cool where he would sit and clean eggs, weigh them, and put them in cartons to take them to sell at the market.
Of course in the winter he cleaned the eggs in the kitchen with Grandma's help. I was so excited when in one of the letters Granddad tells about building the cave.

We would climb trees and play in the hay and ride on the tractor. There were many times we got in trouble because my grandma was always afraid we were going to get hurt. For example, I liked the pigs because there were new baby piglets, so I ventured out by myself one day and climbed the fence to investigate the new babies. I can't even remember if I saw any piglets but what I do remember is what happened at dinner. My grandma had given me an old wrist watch. I don't know if it worked but I loved it and wore it everywhere. Suddenly, I discovered that my watch was missing and thought maybe I lost it in the pig pen. I got up from the table to run back and find it and Granddad said, "Whoa there, where are you going?" I told him about losing the watch in the pig pen and oh my, did I get it. Grandma spoke louder than I ever had heard her before and said, "You should never get in the pen when there are babies. You could have been killed by the mother trying to protect those piglets." I was not allowed to go there alone again but my uncle went up there and found my watch.

My granddad was also the Tax Collector and Justice of the Peace. I remember there were times when people came to the house and we were not allowed in his office. He had a huge oak roll top desk by the fireplace. I loved to sit by him and play with all the interesting things on the desk, in the drawers and cubbyholes.

My grandma was the best cook ever. Her chicken dinners were fabulous. I remember my grandfather catching the chickens and preparing them for Grandma to roast for our dinner. I was happy when the corn was ready to pick because Grandma had a special way of fixing it that cannot compare to anything prepared today. Everything was so fresh and good, food from farm to table.

Grandma and Granddad went to a little country church called Zion Baptist Church. Grandma played the piano for the services. This church was a very important part of their lives before and after their marriage. Zion is referred to many times in the letters. There is a cemetery behind the church where many of my ancestors are buried along with many who are mentioned in the letters. Their names are familiar to me because we went to Zion in the summer. In later years all the roads in the area were given the name of the local families. Of course the road going through the farm was named Patterson Road.

For 28 years my husband Frank and I had a vacation trailer parked at Bear Run Campground in Portersville which is only about five miles from the farm. We traveled all around the Butler County area for years. I became very familiar with all the little towns mentioned in the letters and traveled the same roads that Granddad traveled in his horse and buggy. As I read I could envision where they were going and who they were talking about.

***

5

Some letters are full of information and sweet sayings while other are very boring with weather reports and small talk. Most of the letters start with, "I will endeavor to answer your welcomed letter "or "It is nine o'clock and I have just received your letter and I was exceedingly glad to hear from you." The closings are generally the same, "I guess I will close now hoping to hear from you soon. Give my regards to all inquiring friends. I remain 'As Ever' Your true friend." Because of repetition I have left out many of these opening and closing sentences.

It has been arduous at times to transcribe the letters because some words are faded and hard to read but I have done my best. Some names of people mentioned may be spelled incorrectly due to these difficulties. I have numbered the letters, included the name of who is writing it, and the date and place. When I write direct quotes from the letters they are in *italics* so you will see the original grammar and spelling to reflect the true intent and linguistics of their time. The underlined words in *italics* are also from the original letters

As you read this account of their courtship, you can make up your own mind, but I found my grandfather to be a very gentle, romantic, and spiritual man. Grandmother was independent and confident and also trusted in the Lord. It was difficult to return to this century after reading these letters and I pray that you will enjoy them as much as I have.

Patterson Farm

CHAPTER 1

BEGINNINGS

There is no record of how Frank and Martha met one another. They probably had mutual friends. As young people, friendships were very important as you will see throughout the letters. The letters begin with Frank's simple request to see Martha and her answer yes. This was the beginning of a relationship and long courtship that weathered distance and time. There are only a few letters in 1901 since she had not yet moved a distance away. It is wonderful that they had this time period to get to know one another and establish the relationship that would continue through the letters.

1.   Frank - Aug. 20, 1901, Jacksville, Pa.

Miss Mattie Covert, Rose Point, Pa.
Dear Friend, Pardon me for addressing you without permission, but may I have the pleasure of your company some evening in the near future?
Please be so kind as to send a reply, and if favorable, name a date any time will suit me, so far as I know, except Saturday Aug.24, as I am obliged to remain at home that evening. Hoping to receive a favorable reply I close.

It seems that a letter was the proper way to ask for a date in the early 1900's. I marveled at this lovely and polite introduction with a request for a visit and the pleasure of her company in the near future. After reading this first letter, I was hooked, putting myself back in another century. Frank addresses her as "Miss Mattie Covert" but I never see this again in any letters. He always addressed her as Martha.

2.   Martha - Aug. 26, 1901, Rose Point, Pa.

Mr. Frank Patterson
Dear Friend,
You will have to pardon me for not answering sooner for I was not at home when your letter came. I will except the pleasure of your company next Wednesday eve the 28th if it suits you, as I will not be at home the latter part of the week. So if it suits you, it will be all right.
I will close.
Yours respectfully
Martha Covert

She wrote from the Stone House and accepted his request to visit her Wednesday evening Aug 28, 1901, their first date.

3. Martha - Aug 29, 1901, Rose Point, Pa.

As I promised to write to you if I did not go to town. I will do so now. I did not go to town this week so I will look for you down Saturday eve.

I Just got home from giving one of my pupils a music lesson. My brother and I went to that picnic yesterday we had a fine time.

Martha was a piano teacher. She studied music at Waynesburg College in West Virginia. She taught music to many boys and girls through the years.

Well I will have to close as I must get this to the office or you will not get it this week. Now I will look for you Sat. eve.

There are no more letters from 1901. Apparently they were able to see one another without writing letters. Martha was still living in the Stone House in Rose Point but a letter was still best to make arrangements for a visit.

4. Frank - Feb.4, 1902, Jacksville, Pa.

The new year has arrived and all the holiday festivities are over. Frank is making arrangements to visit her again on Friday.

I will be down or up which ever way you call it on Friday eve. instead of Thursday eve as there is an institute at Harlansburg that eve. (Fri.) and you might care to attend. Tell your Sister, the Fire-keeper , that she can accompany us if she wishes, providing she will continue to keep good fires.

Harlensburg is a small town at the corner of routes PA 108 and US 19. There is not much left in this old town other than a lovey old house that was made into a restaurant many years ago but frequently changes ownership. There is also a gas station and market and the Unity Baptist Church. I imagine the Institute is some kind of Christian meeting.

There are no more letters for seven months.

5.   Martha - Sept. 7, 1902, Rose Point, Pa.

This letter is post marked New Castle, PA, which is about fifteen miles away from Frank. Martha moved in with her sister.

I had a letter from Minta last week "she said" you got home all right, she is talking of coming back in here to work.

I guess I will stay in all winter. I am teaching now. I have five scholars all ready and the promise of more So I think I would rather stay in here than go to Virginia. That is to far from home.

I would like to go out home next Saturday evening. Can't you come in and I will go out with you? Write right a way and let me know whether you will be in or not for if you don't come I will half to find some other way of going, I would like very much if you could come in but if you can-not come in, why I do not want to make it inconvenient for you.

What are you doing these days. I was out at camp meeting yesterday. My Sister and I went out and I met May Kelly out there, So I stayed till evening there. They are having a glorious time.

Well, I guess I will close for this time. Is Sam still at you place yet, if he is give him my best regards. I hope he isn't mad at me yet.

I am not certain who Minta and Sam are, but they may be cousins, Minta on Martha's side and Sam on Frank's. We see news of them included in many letters.

New Castle was a bustling city in Lawrence County. It was a place to go shopping, catch a train, or conduct business. "In the 1870s it was a major hub of the railroad and in the early 1900s the population was about 30,000. Italian immigrants, laborers in nearby limestone quarries, were frequent victims of the Black Hand Society, which employed blackmail and extortion to rob the workers of their pay."[1] When I read this I had to chuckle because the rumor is there are Mafia ties in New Castle to this day.

6.   Frank - Sept. 10, 1902, Slippery Rock, Pa.

Since I saw you I have dug some coal and have been working on top of the ground since last Friday. I was helping to winmill oats yesterday and today I was cutting shingle bolts. Sam is still here.

Windmilling oats and cutting shingle bolts are two functions I am not familiar with but apparently they are farm chores.

Frank tells an interesting account about the horses.

I was in town last Sat. but did not have time to go up to see you. We expected to but bought a horse and while we looked at 6 or 7 we did not get one until Mon. We bought a three year old colt. It is a fine one an iron gray. She has been worked but a few times and has been drove in the buggy but twice, yesterday and today by Sam & me. She went fine, I'll call her Polly. We are going to buy another 3 year old bay tomorrow. I will take Polly to the shop tomorrow.

Horses are very important and Frank includes many accounts about them. Sad to say, that in my memories of the farm there were no horses or buggies, only a 1949 black Chevy and of course a Farmall tractor.

---

[1]Wikipedia.org

Frank adds a little gossip.

Mint is working at Jim Browns now. Alice has the grip. Jim Winer can get another grip now as he is hap its a girl. It arrived Sun. last, not seven months, so you see he has lost no time. I'll bet he takes more time next time.

The gripe or grip is probably a stomach virus or flu. I can only imagine what he is saying about Jim Winer, maybe a baby girl came in only seven months after they were married.

I can not be down after you though much I would like, Sat. Eve on account of my horse having to go in the wagon. So you will not get to ride behind him unless you go down to W.E. Pattersons grocery about 4 P.M.

Young Peoples society was started last Sun. night. Nora I. Pres. Carrol W. V. Pres. Margaret E. Sec F.V.P. treas. Got 71¢ col for a start. I was appointed leader for next Sun. night.

I am sorry I cant go after you but I hope I may get to see you. Write soon as we have got our new mail box. I got your letter in it first. I think of you very often and I only send you one epistle as that was all you sent me.

This letter was signed *"Your true friend and lover."* He is certainly making his feeling known. He is diverting her attention away from the fact he was in town and bought a horse and did not visit her.

CHAPTER 2

ONE YEAR

It is a little over a year since their first date and now they express their feelings without hesitation. She hasn't moved far away, so they have been able to see one another often, building their relationship.

7.   Martha - Sept. 16, 1902, New Castle, Pa.

It sounds like Martha puts a guilt trip on him.

I was very much disappointed Sunday. Thought you would come over to see me, but I guess you don't care to see me any more [sic], but I think of you the same as I always did any way if you don't think of me.

It seems she needs more reassurance of his feelings for her but changes the subject fast by saying she likes it there.

I like teaching in here very much, I don't have to drive like I did out home. It will be much nicer in here in the winter.

8.   Frank - Sept. 22, 1902, Slippery Rock, Pa.

14

To Martha, my dear Sweetheart.

He starts this letter by reassuring her of his feelings. He must have been to New Castle to visit her.

I got home OK. This morning about 2 o'clock. I did not get lost or get off the road. I took a few cat-naps.

There were no street lights or headlights for this 15 mile journey at night in horse and buggy. Then he says,

Nora Dambaugh has captured a fellow that's as ugly as an old mud fence so I am told. I was painting the cracky wagon today. I expect to dig coal tomorrow.

Your sister will think I am a great one as I have eaten two meals there and never even said thanks, explain to her if you think necessary. She will be tempted to say soon that that young Patterson has two uncles and a whole lot of cousins yet he delights to sponge off of us.

He shows such a light-hearted sense of humor. He makes me smile even today over a hundred years later. I never knew that side of him when I was a little kid.

9.   Martha - Sept. 24, 1902, New Castle, Pa.

I have read Tempest and Sunshine through and I think the most of Sunshine, she was true and innocent all through and Tempest was not. Tempest changed some in the end, but she was to deceitful to suit me, so I think the most of Sunshine. You said you thought the most of Tempest when you write, tell me in what way you thought the most of her.

It is a delight for me to see what they were reading in 1902. I bought the book, "TEMPEST AND SUNSHINE" by Mary J.

Holmes to read for myself. The book is difficult to read with small print and no page numbers. The story takes place in Kentucky and portrays life in a small southern town with race and gender issues.

10.   Frank - Sept. 28, 1902, Slippery Rock, Pa.

I expect Sam back tomorrow. I drove Polly to the Point yesterday, she will make a fine buggy horse. I also rode Billy to Jacksville in the afternoon he did well for his first trip.

When Frank talks about going to Jacksville it is humorous to me because when I would ride around that area in the 80's & 90's there were a few houses and no stores. I would see a rather large sign along Rt. 19 that said "Jacksville, Population 52." The sign never changed!

You would be at least two cents better off when you received my last letter. I was disturbed when writing it and put things away rapidly and when I sealed the envelope I discovered I had put my stamp inside.

We had no church today but will have from now on regularly, the young peoples society got twenty six cents tonight.

11.　　Frank - Oct. 1, 1902, Slippery Rock, Pa.

It is after nine o'clock now and I have just received your letter and I was exceeding glad to hear from you as I have been working all day in sight of your home. I was at Moors gathering apples, gathered about 25 bu. And have another days work. While working my mind was on you very often.

Oh how lovely he writes to Martha as she is on his mind so often. He and Sam went to Harlensburg and Sam is going to see May for church Sunday evening.

Grant Studebaker is to be buried tomorrow, typhoid fever cause of his death, I expect to go to the funeral. He is to be buried at Plain Grove.

In early 1903 there was a typhoid epidemic in Butler where over one hundred people died. It was interesting how casual Frank said that Grant Studebaker died of typhoid.

I have not dug any coal for a week and will not this week. We are going to kill a pig tomorrow. Minta wrote home that she was going to surprise you by a visit Sabbath but I guess she would be the one to be surprised.

Now for some gossip.

A young Funkhouser was arrested last Friday for being to good to Del Wimer of Harlensburg. She is the proud mother of a 8 # kid girl. He is 15 and she is 16 years."

CHAPTER 3

WESTON

Martha is still home in Pennsylvania but breaks the news to Frank that she will will be moving to Weston, West Virginia. This begins a new chapter in their romance. Frank has no idea a separation will start that will last many months. He will not have his sweet Martha by his side and will have to continue to look at the Stone House and think of her.

This must have been a very hard letter for her to write. They were able to see one another when she lived in New Castle but now she is moving many miles away.

This begins the bulk of the letters. They must continue their relationship by way of the United States Mail.

Stone House

12.　　Martha - Oct. 1, 1902

This letter is from *"At Home,"* the Stone House in Rose Point.

I am home today. [From New Castle] *Came yesterday afternoon and will stay till tomorrow. I did not know that I was going to be here tonight or I would of let you knowed.* [sic] *For I expect this will be the last time I will be home for a while. I am sorry to tell you that I am going to leave New Castle. I am going to Weston W.Va. Laura's husband came after me and he says he won't go home without me. He has offered me such a good chance that I hate to refuse him. He has offered me far more than I could make all winter in N. C.* [New Castle] *And I am just going to stay till spring.*

Now this is all very unexpected and I would like awful well to see you again before I go. He intends to start back Friday on the nine o'clock train. So I wont get to see you unless you come into New Castle tomorrow. Thurs eve. I think you will get this in time to start in if you have no other arrangements. I would like awful well to see you again.

For I don't suppose I will get to see you for a long, long time again. I will look for you in tomorrow eve. I have something to tell you when I see you. I wish I could of let you knowed then you could of come here tonight. But I did not know every thing. If I would not

19

happen to see you again, why I will write to you when I get to Weston and tell you my offer and all about it. But I hope I may see you though. I can tell you better.

She seems excited about this opportunity, even though it came quickly. Her heart is torn because she wants to see him before she leaves.

Now Frank I guess I have told you all and I expect you will begin to think I have told you enough. But I think it is for the best, and I expect I will never get the chance to go again. So I thought I would go and try it.

I told my Sister what you said in your last letter about not thanking her, she just laughed and said it was all right as long as you could live on the grub.

She pleads one more time.

You come in tomorrow if you possibly can.

She closes with "Love and K", her way of easing the pain of this news since it is not her usual way of closing a letter.

Weston, West Virginia was about 175 miles away so I am sure this was a shock to Frank. We will never know if he made it to New Castle to see her or not.

13.   Martha - Oct. 6, 1902, Weston, W.Va.

My mother made comments on some of the envelopes when she read them. She explained on this one that Martha is going with Mae to live with her sister, Laura Black. Her story of the trip follows.

I got here all O.K. got here last night about half past two o'clock. I told you when I saw you that we would go Fri. At nine o'clock in the morning But we changed our mind and did not go till Saturday morning. Mae thought we would wait till Sat. morning at five o'clock, and I could see more of the country. But I did not see very much of the country after all.

When we got to New Castle Junction, we had to wait on the train six hours, it was just six hrs late. We didn't get started from there till eleven o'clock, it was half past too, when we got to Pittsburg, So we had two hrs before the train for Weston, so Mae showed me some of Pittsburg. I saw the highest building in the city it was twenty-two stories high. When you would look up you would think it was going to fall on you.

From N.C. Junction, you may as well say I had to stand all the way to Pittsburg. The train had thirteen coaches on and they were all just packed full, it was just simply awful. I never was as tired in my life. You will half to look over the mistakes and poor writing, for I didn't get to bed last night till four o'clock in the morning and I am very tired and sleepy. I promised to write to you today, and I don't like to break a promise.

This was not an easy trip for a young girl. It was good her sister and Mr. Black were with her.

I have used the spelling of Pittsburg as Frank and Martha did. "The city was named for William Pitt and originally was called Pittsbourgh in 1758. In the city charter, granted on March 18, 1816, the Pittsburgh spelling is used on the original document, but due to an apparent printing error, the 'Pittsburg' spelling is found on official copies of the document printed at the time. Over several years there was much debate of the correct spelling and on July 19, 1911 the 'H' in Pittsburgh was restored."[2]

---

[2]From Visit Pittsburgh.com "The Pittsburgh "H"

As for the country I can't tell you anything about it, it was pretty near dark when we left Pitts that I did not get to see anything. I don't know whether I will like this place or not. I haven't seen very much of it yet. But it is not a very big place. I will tell you later on what I think of the place when I get to see more of it.

Now Frank I guess I will close for this time, as it is bed time. I will try and write more next time.
O, yes I forgot to ask you if you missed one of your handkerchief, you left one the last night you was over. It is at home if you want it, you can call there for it. I got your letter that was waiting on me when I went to N.C.[New Castle]

14.	Frank - Oct. 12, 02, Slippery Rock, Pa.

Your letter was received this eve. I have just come from church and will write a few lines in answer tonight. Three - Emma Davis - Hanna Winers and Frank English have been received for baptism during the meetings. They are to continue this week at least.
I have taught but one this last month in S.S. [Sunday School] *being absent the other times. I expect to be on hand for a while now. Some had quit coming since day school begun.*

Frank is very involved in his church. He has held various positions including Sunday school teacher.

Last Sabbath Margaret and I got up and started for Girard O. at six o'clock. We got to New Castle at eight and left on the street car for Youngstown at 9:15. When we got to Y - we had to wait for about an hour before Miss Weiner came and then we left for Girard. And after looking at pictures and getting our dinner we started out for a walk to where a new RR was being built after walking over two high RR bridges and some uneven ground also on the steel rails of RR tracks (for about 5 or 6 Mile.) We arrived at our starting place had a lunch and started for home.

22

Youngstown, Ohio, is about twenty miles from New Castle and Girard about five more miles. It is interesting that they traveled by way of a streetcar and not a train. I found a very interesting article about the streetcars in New Castle.

"While urban streetcar systems blossomed in such places as New Castle and Youngstown, a host of 'interurban' streetcar lines were established to connect them all together. In late 1901 the New Castle & Lowellville Street Railway Company began work on an interurban line to Lowellville, which then connected with another line and continued on to Youngstown and Warren. This line, known as the 'Lowellville Line,' ran from along the north bank of the Mahoning River and made a stop in rural Edinburg. In about May 1902 this line was merged with the New Castle streetcar system and consolidated under the new Pennsylvania & Mahoning Valley Railway Company."[3]

Miss Sadie has two grown sisters and a whole lot of small brothers. They have a piano with a mandolin attached which gives excellent music but as they are just learning they can't play much yet. During our walk the two sisters obtained fellows which I judge must have been watching for them and of course I wondered if there could be any chance for me to gain any love until and it not until we were ready to start to home that my dreams were shattered, for Miss Winers was going so far as Youngstown with us a journey a young man stepped out of the darkness and went along. However I am not sorry for I think I have better prospects in Weston.

He finishes the letter the next day with some more interesting small talk.

Sam is still here and will be only the rest of the week. He is at the height almost of his ambition now for he was at a dance at

[3] lawrencecountymemoirs.com/New Castle Electric Street Railway Company - New Castle PA

Jacksville hall last Friday. I judge from his talk that it is not the dance he cares for so much as it is the feeling and desires that comes to all who partake of the worldly sport. Remember ballroom to him he thinks Mabel Mae are to slow and bashful for him now and if continues as he talks she will no doubt get what he wants if not more.

There is so much small talk in these letters about who is going with whom. But one thing for sure, Frank and Martha looked down upon ballroom dancing.

15.   Martha - Oct. 12, 1902, Weston, W.Va.

I just got through writing a letter to Minta. I am very sorry I shall surprise her so, but it cannot be help't. When you said you was working in sight of home, it made me think of home. All though I think I will like this place after I get acquainted.

But you see some queer looking people here. It is not near as big a place as New Castle is. It has no street cars or any thing of that kind. There is a big asylum here, there is eleven hundred patients in it. It is one mile long so you may know it is a very large building. I just wish you could see the hills here. You would say there was know hills out there, to compare with these.

The Trans Allegheny Lunatic Asylum is located in Weston, West Virginia. After being closed in the the 1980s, it is now open for tours. At the time of this letter the hospital was designed for 250 patients had over a thousand. It was interesting to read about it.

"The hospital was intended to be self-sufficient, and a farm, dairy, waterworks, and cemetery were located on its grounds, which ultimately reached 666 acres in area. A 1938 report by a survey committee organized by a group of North American medical organizations found that the hospital housed "epileptics, alcoholics, drug addicts and non-educable mental defectives" among its population."[4]

Martha refers to this hospital in several letters.

16.   Frank - Oct. 15, 1902, Slippery Rock, Pa.

When I wrote last I said I was going to Grants funeral. Well I went there was a very large crowd and among the chief mourners was the young lady from below Pittsburg to whom he was engaged. I felt especially sorry for her.

---

[4]Wikipedia

You will no doubt notice that this is not written very good the following is the cause.

I have a bone-felon or a sore called a catarrh on the third finger of my right hand. It began to get sore last Friday and on Mon. Eve. I had it lanced I have got a considerable amount of matter out. I do not expect it to be sore long although I have heard of them being painful for two months or more. They are caused by a bruise. I was digging coal when mine started. I have not dug any since and will not until this gets entirely well. So don't worry.

He continues about Sam.

Sam told me he went to see Mary last Sun. Eve. and saw her going to milk and then his courage failed him and he did not speak the burden of his heart. However he says he wrote her a letter so we must wait developments.

Margarets birthday was last Mon. She was 20. Sams is Saturday coming. I got him a mouth organ to commemorate it by.

17.   Martha – Oct. 19, 1902, Weston, W.Va.

She explains that she had just gotten home from Sunday School.

I was at church this morning and they have Sunday School in the afternoon.

This is a beautiful day. We all intended to take a drive out in the country today, but we could not get a rig in town they were all out. This is the only Sunday Mae will be home for a while and he wanted to take us out driving so I could see the country. But we had to stay at home. He [Mr. Black] starts to work in the morning and will not be home for two or three weeks.

She is sorry about Frank's sore finger and adds a warning.

26

You had better stay out of that mine or you will get killed next.

She has a cold now and attributes it to the move to the South and change of climate. She says it is a beautiful day so Martha and her sister went for a walk down the street. They walked around the asylum because it is *"it is simply a fine place, it is just like a park around it."* Martha has been in Weston for a couple of weeks and is very curious about her surroundings.

18. Frank - Oct. 21, 1902, Slippery Rock, Pa.

His hand is almost better so he is going to dig coal tomorrow.

There was a party at Frank Books last Friday evening. I was there the principal guest was a Miss Kate Book of Tennessee. I think every one had a good time and also a good lunch. Sam & Mae were out at Zion Sunday night I have had lots of fun since as Sam lost his knee spread going to church. I found it and have found out since that they came near up setting.

I am expecting to dig coal day after tomorrow. Now don't worry about me as I am going to, if its Gods will, come out of the Humble Mine OK.

In my curiosity of the history of the time I tried to find out about the Humble Mine but to no avail. I also tried to find out what a knee spread is but cannot locate any information. I wondered if it was a blanket over their knees but I can't figure out what that has to do with "up setting."

Sam brought his crokinole board up Mon. We played Mon. Eve 3 games. I beat him each time.

I was excited to learn about this game. At first I thought I was reading it wrong because I never heard of this. But when I entered it into the computer I learned the following.

"The first board was built by Eckhardt Wettlaufer in 1876 in Ontario. ... It quickly became popular in Amish and Mennonite communities in Southern Ontario, possibly because it was seen as a less sinful past time than dancing or card playing".[5]

Incidentally, there is a large Amish community about 15 miles from the farm. The game is played on a round board about 36 inches in diameter with a small hole in the middle with strategic posts around it. One must flick a little disc into the hole.

There are interesting rules to the game such as the one cheek rule, which says, "One butt cheek must always touch the chair."[6] It is still played today including world championship games. I thought I should buy one and try it out but they start at $149 dollars on Amazon.

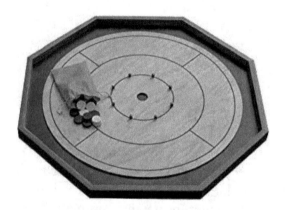

Wednesday Frank says he will steal enough time to finish his letter.

We are building a new cave the walls are to be 5 ft. High. The stone masons are working at it today."

---

[5]Wikipedia
[6]Complete Rules of Crokinole by Erik Arneson

Adalina Covert, Martha's mother.

CHAPTER 4

CHURCH

Martha and Frank spent a great deal of time detailing church activities because that was such an important part of their lives.

19.   Martha - Oct. 27, 1902, Weston, W.Va.

Sabbath is my busiest day, and I guess I will have to put off writing till Mon. I am at the church about all day you might say, At church in the morning and Sabbath school in the afternoon and choir practice after Sabbath. As I have the honor of being a member of the choir. They invited me in it, and at church in the evening. So you see how it is. They have quite a large choir there is twelve in it. We meet once through the week to practice too. I have got acquainted with quite a number of the good people of the church.

This is followed by much small talk. Martha always asks for information about the people back home. She knows their friends are dating and it was important for her to know who was with whom.

20.   Frank - Oct. 28, 1902, Slippery Rock, Pa.

The cave was finished on Oct. 24, 1902 and Frank describes it very simply.

It has stone walls, roof of chestnut posts and covered with dirt.

When I was growing up and went to the farm this cave was covered with grass and had to be mowed to keep it decent looking. It was built on a slight slope of the land so the door was on the downward side of the slope. If you were on the outside on top of the cave, there was about a six or seven foot drop to the ground. Grandma worried we would fall off and told us not to be on top of the cave. Did we listen to her? Too much fun to roll down the side.

Frank talks about his dreams for Martha.

Reno did not arrive here as was expected, but I went to Uncles anyway. I enjoyed myself as well as I expected but I thought of you very often while there, for if I thought you would be such a wife I would be tempted not to write any more but I have high hopes of your ability. I will explain more fully in the future.

It is lovely that he tells her that he is thinking about her so often and even as a wife.

For the first time this summer, I and my cousin Dewit, rode wheels about 8 mi. there & back, to the coal mines while I was not in them yet I would rather work in our own.

I believe that when he says they, "rode wheels", he is talking about an automobile. There are interesting pictures of 1902 automobiles on the internet. http://earlyamericanautomobiles.com/1902.htm.

He continues with much small talk, but always, what was happening at church.

There is nothing going on Halloween around here that I know of except church at Zion for three nights, Wed, Thurs., and Fri. this week. I was not there tonight.

Frank wants to know more about Weston so he asks questions.

After meeting so many pleasant people, do you think you will really want to come back to Penna. [sic] when your vacation time comes? What church do you go to? Are you teaching music? Do you ever get homesick or lovesick? What is the climate like? Do you get tired of questions?

Isn't it romantic that he says "lovesick"?

32

21.   Martha - Nov 2, 1902, Weston, W. Va.

I will resolve to answer some of the questions in your letter. In regard to what church I go too. I go to the Methodist Church. Don't you think that is right to always follow up your own denomination? I have a few music scholars. I am not as successful as I hoped for, but there is time enough yet. I have to get a little acquainted first and if it is God's will I shall succeed in getting more.

In regard of home, I think of home very often and also of <u>you</u>. But I have to banish all thoughts of getting homesick because it will do know [sic] good. My Sister is very good to me in which it keeps me from getting homesick. But my memory often runs back to this time last year. What makes you think I wont want to go back to Penna? I think I shall be ready to go back when spring comes. All though I have met some very nice people that wont keep me from going back home.

I have joined a sewing circle that is for a short time. It is for the church they are going to have a rummage sale, they are going to sell all second hand things, and things that you need to remedy in any way. The ladies of the church meets and mends them. When they get all this done they will have a sale. They are trying to raise money enough to build a new church. I think it will be very interesting work. We meet tomorrow afternoon for the first.

I love that my grandmother wrote that even though she was not so busy with her students, she kept from being homesick with her involvement with church and family. This shows me that she is a practical and strong woman at this young age. She has answered many of Frank's questions.

22.   Frank - Nov. 5, 1902, Slippery Rock, Pa.

I am really a citizen of the U.S. now for I cast my first vote

33

yesterday.
This is what was happening at the time politically.

"The 1902 United States elections elected the 58th United States Congress, [which] occurred in the middle of Republican President Theodore Roosevelt's first term, during the Fourth Party System. Roosevelt had become president on September 14, 1901, upon the assassination of his predecessor, William McKinley. Republicans retained a majority in both chambers of Congress, while the Populist Party and Silver Republican Party disappeared from Congress."[7]

I am much pleased to learn that you are making use of your talents in church work away down in W. Va. As to what church you should go, do as you think God would have you do. I would be pleased to be there awhile to help you.

Frank gives details about a party that Sam went to and then add these sweet words.

I cannot think of much to write but if I were to write all the thought of you that passes through my mind at times I could keep you busy for a while reading.

Thurs. Since writing the last I have found that I am to go to N. C. [New Castle] two weeks from next Sat or on Nov.22 as Father & Mother are invited to a golden wedding of S. H. Moors.

I am digging coal today I have been making from $1.00 to $2.00 each day I work.

I think of you very often and always remember you in my prayers and hope you do me also. I am your own true friend that awaits a reply.

---

[7]Wikipedia "United States Elections, 1902"

23. Martha - Nov. 9, 1902, Weston W.Va.

I thought I would sit down and write you a few lines till Church time. It is not like it was at home, I would sit down and wait on you to come and go along to C. [church] but I can not do that now, so I will do the next best.

Do you still teach your S.S. [Sunday School] *class? And how are you getting a long with it? I wish to you could be here for a while. I would like to see your <u>smiling face</u>.*

There was a young lady died just the third house below us, with typhoid fever. There is a great deal of fever here now.

I had a letter from Minta yesterday the same time I rec'd yours. She seems to be as happy as a bee, by the way she wrote. She said she heard you was coming down to Weston W.Va. But I guess she made that up herself. I would be much pleased to see you, but I am afraid you would not take that notion. She said she just wished I was N.C. [New Castle] *instead of W.Va. But I left it with Him who knowth all things best.*

I was at Church and we heard a very good sermon this eve. They have a good preacher too. The best of it is, he is a single man too. I expect he weighs two hundred, he is a good preacher all the same.

She closes her letter with this keeping in mind their beautiful connection though the Lord.

I always remember you in my prayers and glad to know you do the same with me.

It warms my heart to know that these two young people would be praying for each other during their separation.

24.   Martha - Nov. 17, 1902, Weston, W.Va.

She is helping the church organist plan a church supper which will be held next Thursday. Then she relays this interesting bit.

We had company all day yesterday. You heard me speak of that young man last winter that got his fingers taken off here. It was him and his girl and her sister that was here. It seems like such a pity for him.

You know Uncle Jim Wilson that was with us all last winter, is dead. We will not see him any more in this world. I often think now that we did not know when he left us for his home in the west that we would never see him again. But it is Gods will, not ours. He just left for his home in July. So he has not been at home a great while till he was called to that home on high.

She expresses her faith when relating this sad bit of news. She changes the subject to this interesting news.

There has been a great deal of robbery done in this town the last couple weeks. They have not bothered us yet. They had better not or I will shoot them. You know how well I can shoot a revolver. They have not caught them yet. There are guards watching for them but it seems they can't catch them. They have been in several of houses around. But there is a gas light in the front and one in the back of our house. So I expect it is to light for them here.

I never saw or heard about any guns at the farm and absolutely cannot imagine Grandma shooting one! I believe she has a sense of humor.

25.   Frank - Nov. 19, 1902, Slippery Rock, Pa.

He is writing this to *"cheer her heart."* So much of this letter is centered around the Lord, from Sunday school to baptisms.

I have just come from church where there was a prayer meeting and a study of S.S. [Sunday School] *lesson for next Sabbath. Emma Davis, Hannah Wimer, Arona Pounds and Frank English were buried with Christ in Baptism last Sun. I was sorry to hear that 'Uncle Jim' had been called home. I often think of his favorite piece of music "Holy City."*

In your last letter you asked if I were coming down. I don't know until the time comes to start but how would you like to have me come like "the thief in the night"– unexpected. However I don't expect to stay on for a good while yet, as I expect to get some sheep and that will take my "loose" change and I am not digging much coal and may not for a few days yet as "Dad" has been on the sick list with a carbuncle on his hip but it is getting well now.

He makes a sweet reference to Martha in closing.

I am all alone now when in bed since Sam has gone but I sometimes dream of you so I don't miss him. I am going to town Sat. and I hope you may have something to be thankful for on next Thurs. I must close for this time again send my love and I do hope you will not eat to much at the feast tonight. I am going to help set the slack burner in the room now. Yours as ever and forever if you wish.

CHAPTER 5

THE GIFT

26.   Martha - Nov. 24, 1902, Weston, W.Va.

Frank sent her a gift but nowhere does it say what it is.

I received the gift without the point this evening and I thank you many, many times for it. For I think it is just beautiful and it is just the fit I was not looking for it quite so soon. I soon discovered it was from when I saw the initials on it. I think it is a very nice gift, and I shall commend it very highly.

She was a server at the church dinner on Thursday and they made $75.00 and could have made a $100.00 but ran out of food. Then on Saturday they had an ice cream social were she was a server again. She was happy that four people chose the right path at Zion (the ones who got baptized).

Say Frank, if you have any notion of coming out any time, I would be very much pleased if you would let me know before you come. It will be two months next Sat. since I came to Weston. I like the place very much. I have not got home-sick yet; but I am getting anxious for I have not heard from home, for over two weeks. In the last letter Father was not very well and I thought perhaps he was worse and they did not want to let me know it. But I hope for a letter soon. This has been a very disagreeable day it has been raining all day. It is very cold too. I think it is going to snow.

27.   Frank - Nov. 28, 1902, Slippery Rock, Pa.

He was pleased to know she liked the gift. But what was it?

I hope it may never be used by anyone for dishonorable purposes.

Frank shows his interest in Godly matters when and expresses it often.

I received a letter from Rev. Nelson today. He has been preaching and doing pastoral work for seven weeks, for three of those weeks he was 175 miles from home and the rest he has been at his church Cedar Falls Ia. During the past month 28 have been baptized 4 received by letter as experience and some more baptisms next Sabbath.

Mother was troubled with rheumatism for a day or two and I had to help be girl in morning and evening. She is some better now.

He must have meant he had to help out with inside chores rather than farm work.

If I thought it would do any good I would try and make you homesick. I often look across the fields and have thoughts which cannot be written.

I had a letter from Miss Fanny McBride whom you met at Cascade Park in behalf of the Y.W.C.T.U. She asked for a handkerchief to be used at a handkerchief bazaar. She said it did not matter what kind or size so I got a large bandanna and put a nice one of a smaller size inside so you can see I am a temperance nice worker.

39

Y.W.C.T.U. stands for Young Women's Christian Temperance Union. I remember when I was a little girl hearing about my grandmother being involved with the W.C.T.U.

28.   Martha - Dec. 2, 1902, Weston, W.Va.

It was four days since Martha received a letter so she said that she thought it was late due to a train wreck in New Castle. She read about in it the paper and was worried that the letter was on that train. She says the following in response to his last letter.

I am very glad to know that you are a Temperance worker as well as a Christian worker. And I hope you will always remain such. For you know what God said in Prov. 20:1?

That verse says, "Wine is a mocker, strong drink a brawler, and whoever is led astray by it is not wise."

Frank I did not fully understand what you mentioned in your letter in regard to the gift not to be used for dishonorable purposes, I would like for you to explain in the next letter. Would you think that I would use it that way?

Hmm, what in the world was that gift? I am still not sure what it was.

29.   Frank - Dec. 5, 1902, Slippery Rock, Pa.

We have been butchering some today killed two hogs and have been helping make sausage tonight.

Sam was up last evening to invite me to a party at their place tomorrow night. I don't know much about it as I did not see him.

Last Sabbath eve. Miss Morgan a retuned missionary from Siam (or some place) gave a very interesting talk on missions she is raising money to return I have heard.

In regard to the sentence in regard to the dishonorable use of things, don't worry your head about it as it has no reference to you and was not of much value.

I have just dug 130 bu of coal this week besides 40 bu for ourselves. I won't dig much if any next week as Father is a jury man at Butler.

He did not get the letter finished until Saturday and then he finished it.

I was at the party last night. I think all enjoyed themselves as well as usual at such gatherings. There was thirty some there, the usual crowd. Ed Miller had his fiddle there so there was plenty of music for skip and reel the willow. Mae was there. I did not get much time to talk to her. She said your father was not feeling very well. I did not get the particulars.

I find it interesting that the *"skip and reel the willow"* is an acceptable dance. In my research I find that there was a jig called "Strip the Willow" and it was much like a square dance that I learned in grade school. My conclusion is that ballroom dancing, mentioned previously, is forbidden but square dancing is fine.

We had a very heavy snow here Thursday night. It is melting some now.

My love to you is still the same, but don't you think one often runs a great risk in loving for we see by the papers that words in Prov. 25:24 often prove true.

Proverbs 25:24 says, "It is better to dwell in the corner of the housetop, than with a brawling woman and in a wide house."

I sure don't know why he quoted such a scripture when he is telling her that he still loves her.

CHAPTER 6

CHRISTMAS

As they approach the Christmas season, it is evident that they will be apart this year. However they do send gifts to one another. The season included many church activities and of course parties with friends.

30.   Martha - Dec. 10, 1902, Weston, W.Va.

She reports that they had a foot of snow and now it is raining so she is not going to prayer meeting.

There was three girlfriends of mine who called last Thurs eve. We had a fine time. They had to hear some music and my sister has a gramophone and we played that. They are all in my S.S. [Sunday School] *class.*

An interesting event is recorded next.

There was a big fire in town yesterday. It was a large residence, there was two families that lived in it. One man lost everything they had. He told Mr. Black he had a notion to get on drunk and stay that way for a week as if that would help him. That has been four fires in this town since I came. I saw one burning. There was

43

four families lived in it. The first fire I ever saw.

Well I guess you will get tired of reading this as I took from your last letter you was getting tired corresponding to me. I read it with that meaning anyway. So I guess I will close for this time, in which I shall look for a reply soon if you wish to write to me anymore.

She just seems so insecure about his love for her. I wonder if it has something to do with the scripture he quoted in the previous letter!

31.   Frank - Dec.14, 1902, Slippery Rock, Pa.

Father was at Butler as juryman all last week. I was very busy from the time he left. I was at town yesterday with the marketing. I sold butter at 34¢, eggs 35¢ per doz. apples 6 for 10¢. The day was extremely bad as it was raining and freezing, the roads were very icy but I got along without any accident. As soon as I finish this I am to take Margaret to Slippery Rock so she can go on the cars to Butler to the institute next week.

The cars may be a train. Butler is about twenty miles from Slippery Rock. It is such a wonderful look at history as we see how much he is selling his farm goods.

Sam's horse is sick. It is some better last report, impaction of the bowels was the ailment. He had a horse doctor from town and it cost him about $11.00. I guess it was getting too much feed and not doing enough.

Frank tries answers her insecurities.

I was greatly surprised when I read that you thought I was tired of corresponding with you. I do not remember what I could have written that could have offended you and as I meant nothing of the kind, I am not going to worry much at the false alarm and I hope you are thinking different by this time. You surely have not have

44

forgotten the promise.

Dear Martha, please remember that if this message of mine appears cold or indifferent please remember it comes from one who loves you.

He does not understand why she is feeling unsure and insecure about his feelings.

32.   Martha - Dec. 16, 1902, Weston, W.Va.

She refers back to there being some words written that may have offended her. Again, could it have been the Bible verse about a brawling woman?

I will not tell you now what you wrote, but probably I will some other time.

Their Christian activities take up much of each letter.

Did you hear of Margaret Dombart's conversion. She has joined the M.E. Church and Epworth League of New Castle. She works at Rev. Parsons.

Last Sun. the Supt. of S.S. [Sunday school] *invited me to teach a class in which I was greatly surprised for there are other girls that have been going longer. But I taught the class of thirteen girls. Do you still have your class yet?*

She continues and asks him about any special plans for Xmas. They usually abbreviate Christmas like this, X being Greek for Christ.

Do you remember last Xmas eve what you said? You wondered where we would be this Xmas. Little did I know then that I would be in Weston. But we do not know one minute what is in store for

45

us the next.

33.   Frank - Dec. 18, 1902, Slippery Rock, Pa.

I received your loving message this afternoon and read it several rods under the ground. I was pleased with it as it appeared to have a different ring to the words than the other. I was digging coal Tues. Wed. and today, Mon. I had to clear the ditch. I have dug over 1600 bu of coal since I started this fall but do not have much to show for it now.

Is he referring to money? Is he not making enough or is he spending what he makes? Then he writes these insightful words.

The older I grow the more I realize that the words of the poet are true. 'Life is real, Life is earnest, And the grave is not the goal'. - etc."

I used his few words and looked them up and and found that he was quoting from a poem. I include the poem to give insight as to what he was reading.[8] It is hard for me to imagine the old rugged farmer that I knew as Granddad, reciting lines from this poem.

A Psalm of Life

Henry Wadsworth Longfellow, 1807 - 1882

What the Heart of the Young Man Said to the Psalmist
Tell me not, in mournful numbers,
"Life is but an empty dream!"
For the soul is dead that slumbers,
And things are not what they seem.

Life is real! Life is earnest!
And the grave is not its goal;

---

[8]From www.poetryfoundation.org

"Dust thou art, to dust returnest,"
Was not spoken of the soul.

Not enjoyment, and not sorrow,
Is our destined end or way;
But to act, that each to-morrow
Finds us farther than to-day.

Art is long, and Time is fleeting,
And our hearts, though stout and brave,
Still, like muffled drums, are beating
Funeral marches to the grave.

In the world's broad field of battle,
In the bivouac of Life,
Be not like dumb, driven cattle!
Be a hero in the strife!

Trust no Future, howe'er pleasant!
Let the dead Past bury its dead!
Act,--act in the living Present!
Heart within, and God o'erhead!

Lives of great men all remind us
We can make our lives sublime,
And, departing, leave behind us
Footprints on the sands of time;

Footprints, that perhaps another,
Sailing o'er life's solemn main,
A forlorn and shipwrecked brother,
Seeing, shall take heart again.

Let us, then, be up and doing,
With a heart for any fate;
Still achieving, still pursuing
Learn to labor and to wait.

He continues his letter with Christian thoughts.

I had not heard of Margaret D. conversion and I hope she may never be tempted to turn back. I am pleased to know you are teaching and hope you may continue, I have not been at S.S. [Sunday School] very regularly for a while and the most of my class has ceased coming since bad weather set in. I am to open the topic in Y.P.S. [Young Peoples Society] on next Sabbath eve. There is pretty good crowds when the weather and roads are good and when they are bad it is the opposite.

I have heard of nothing going on at Xmas. I am exceedingly sorry you are so far away this Xmas. I think of you very often and long for the time when I can again sit by your side. Is it not your desire as well as mine that ere another year passes that we shall be much nearer and dearer to each other? You will be twenty-one then remember!

34.   Frank - Dec. 23, 1902, Slippery Rock, Pa.

I received this evening a token of your love which I highly appreciate. The gift came O.K. with the exception of a slight jar which bent the clasp but that is all right now as I just got through fixing it. It is very beautiful and while one can very well do without such things yet it is what I have for a long time wished for and was not expecting to get.

My mother had also got me a Cuff & Collar Box but as yours came first the other will be exchanged, as it would have been had it came last. It is nice but yours is a great deal nicer.

"Men's historical fashion albeit is not as familiar to most folks as women's fashion of the last 1800's to early 1900's.

"Clothing was handmade back then, which included men's shirts, collars and cuffs. Because clothing was handmade, that made it more expensive. Men would wear undershirts to protect their dress shirts, however the places that had the most body contact in a shirt were at the collar and cuff.

"Thus these were added to preserve a shirt in the places that an undershirt did not protect. It was much more cost efficient to purchase just a collar and a set of cuffs than to purchase the entire shirt with them on. Thus the need for the collar box.

"By removing the collar and cuffs to wash the shirt, made it possible to save on the expense of buying these items because all you had to do was to purchase a new shirt and re-button the collar and cuffs to the new shirt. Collar Boxes were used to keep the collar and cuffs from getting dirty when not being used."[9]

Sam came for a visit and told of entertainment going on in various communities but Frank didn't commit to attending any. He tells her what others are doing.

The preacher's daughter is coming home Xmas and Margaret and Irene invited to a party at the parsonage Friday night. Mint is coming home today to spend Xmas. Sam is going with Pearl Van Horne now. He had her to church Sun night.

He is still having trouble getting to church because of the bad roads, but he got his Sunday School Class a pocket mirror and comb.

35.   Martha - Dec. 25, 1902, Weston, W.Va.

---

[9]From Collectorsweekly.com

I will take the pleasure of writing you a few lines on this Xmas day and thanking you for the beautiful present you sent me. I appreciate it very much for I think it is a very nice present. And I shall take great pleasure in reading it now. I thank you many times for it. I have rec'd quite a number of very nice presents but yours exceeds them all.

She got home from Sunday School where they had collected food for the poor and then gave the kids candy. Then came this colorful description of things happening in town.

Did you ever hear of people shooting guns and crackers and all kinds of explosive things for Xmas? It was just simply awful to be on the street last Tues. eve. They would just throw them at people and under the horses feet. The men They just fooled around til they broke a big show window in a clothing store. So that put a stop to it. The police gave orders and throwed [sic] bills all over town what they would do if they heard any more shooting. So it put a stop to it.

She breaks some hard news to him.

I rec'd your welcome letter last Sun on my birthday. And to the question you ask me in last portion of the letter. I am looking forth for that time when we shall soon meet again. But I am afraid it will be a long time while yet before I shall be at home. For Sister does not know where they will move yet, and they are trying to persuade me to stay another year with them. But if I should make that arrangement I think I shall go home first. But I have not made known promise yet. So I will wait till that time that is till we move.

36. Frank - Dec. 28, 1902, Slippery Rock, Pa.

I received your letter yesterday in which you thanked me for the gift. I knew that a S.S. [Sunday School] teacher especially needed a Bible and it is a thing that can be used every day as well as Sun.

I am happy to know you are pleased with it.

He said that his mother got him a nice lamp in place of the other gift. Mint is home till Tuesday. She got all her upper teeth out but doesn't look too bad. Vincent got her a nice watch chain and Sam went to VanHornes again.

I was at church tonight a good crowd was there. I got invited to a Crokinole party at the hall Thurs night. I was to take a girl but I don't know where to get one yet. You are needed. The party at the preachers was a very good time. The preachers daughter appeared like a nice girl.

I would be exceeding sorry to hear of your promising to staying in Weston for another year and I hope your love for me may help to cause you to refuse. However it is not for me to say what you shall do for you know where the most pleasure of this life is for you.

Frank must come to grips that Martha is thinking of staying in West Virginia for another year. But he may be in denial when he says he hopes she will be home by spring.

37.   Martha - Dec. 31, 1902, Weston W.Va.

I am very glad it know that you are pleased with your gift. I intended to make you a bouquet of the wax flowers. But you cannot send them through the mail and that is reason I did not send them. I feel very sorry I disappointed your mother for I know it would be a disappointment to her. But your letter today started that - the exchange was made all right for the lamp. In which I am very glad it could be exchanged because I felt very sorry I had disappointed your mother so.

I appreciated your gift to me very much. It is some thing I have always wanted and thank you again.

Frank I hope you have found a girl for tomorrow eve by this time. For I know they are not so scarce as that and I hope you have a nice time.

I am invited to the home of one of my girl friends this eve to watch the New Year in, she has several invited in of course it a party. I had a fine time last Mon. eve. Our S.S class met at our teachers home to organize a "Dorcas Circle". It is to help the poor and lend a helping hand to all Christian work. We are to meet every Wed. but after we go through that business. We had music and played games and had refreshments in which was very nice. We all just had a lovely time.

Perhaps you will think that same way. I have spoken here, I am not a teacher. I am not a regular teacher just a supply because I do not want to be a regular teacher for I have such a fine teacher. I would rather be taught than teach. I think that was a very nice gift you gave to your S.S. Class for Xmas.

They are going to commence their revival meeting in our church next Wed. eve. The Baptists are holding there meetings now. I was there last night. They have an evangelist preaching for theirs. He a great singer and player and a fine preacher.

I think I shall be home in the spring if not before that. For I had a letter from Mae and she said Father was not very well and also an aunt which is visiting there has been very poorly. So it makes me a little homesick for I feel I am needed there. But I hope they are all better by this time.

CHAPTER 7

NEW YEAR

38.   Frank - Jan 4, 1903, Slippery Rock, Pa.

The party on Thursday, New Year's Eve went as follows:

I had the pleasure of the company of Olive Studebaker, school begins Tues and she will not be home till June. She expects to finish. There was twenty couple and we played 12 games there was plenty of boards (Crokinole) and they were numbered 1,2,3,4 etc. You were given a number and took your partner to that board. If you beat you went to the next board and changed partners with the one that got beat and so on. Grace Gardner and Lee McCracken won the most games. They were each given a book.
I give you the couples
Wm Roland – Mable Boook
Ray Gardner – Miss Miller - School teacher Zion
Walter Book – Jessie Book
John Davis – Bertha Dambaugh
Harry McCracken – Nora
Lee   McCracken - Ida Gardner
Jimmy McCracken - Mary Gardner
Port Book – Grace Gardner
Ron Studebaker – Emma Davis

Jim Studebaker – Miss Walkers -Sara Hill teacher
Ed Miller – Maude Miller
Clarence Vogan – Miss Douglas
Sid Allison – Miss Douglas
Orange Studebaker – Holly Hickathonn
Roy Humphrey – Nilla Humphrey
Ralph Gardner – Miss Roland -Rev's Daughter
Carrol Williams – Margaret Book
Sam Patterson – Pearl VanHorne
F.V. Patterson – Olive Studebaker
As there was uneven couples Mr. and Mrs. W.F. Gardner was called in and proved better than many others. I helped to win 5 games.
After the play a fine lunch was eaten by all which the girls had wisdom enough to bring.

There was fine sleighing here last week but now there is mud there. Was several at church tonight. I got 77cents collection. I now have 94 cents.

What a wonderful way to spend a New Year's Eve. Lot's of friends and games. And of course food, but no alcohol or craziness. Just good clean old-fashioned fun.

39.   Martha – Jan. 8, 1903, Weston, W.Va.

She starts her letter explaining that she was at the Dorcas Circle which is a missionary society for women. She is the secretary but doesn't like it. She continues about church and other activities.

In the evening I went to the Baptist Church to hear the evangelist, it was his last night here. I think he is fine. There was one more taken in to this church last night.

I was glad to know you had a nice time at the Hall Thur evening. I

54

was at church on that eve. But I was at watch the night before which we had a nice time. There was not a great many there for there was several other things going on that eve. There was a big Ball at the Asylum, a good many went there. You know there are some people would rather attend any thing like that, than to a little party at a private house.

For such a young woman she is very opinionated about what people should be doing. But the asylum is such an interesting place I might have preferred to go there.

This is a very disagreeable day, it is snowing and drifting. We will have sleighing if it keeps on. I can remember the sleigh rides I had last winter which I can thank you for. But I suppose there will some other girl in demand this winter.

I wrote to Minta but she has not answered yet. It looks like her and Victor would soon be made one. Sam's girl, is it that VanHorne girl that Jim Vogan went with?

I have got a very bad cold. I have felt just about half sick all week. I do not know whether it is homesickness or not – but I guess not. Well I will half to close for this time and hope to hear from you soon.

40. Frank - Jan. 11, 1903, Slippery Rock, Pa.

My poetic grandfather responds to her insecurities when she said that she supposes there will be another girl in demand for sleigh rides.

If the snow stays the sleighing will be fine now. But also for me and some other girl you hinted at I can best explain my self in the old song:

My sleigh (canoe) is under cover (water)

55

And my bells (banjo) is unstrung
I am tired of living any more:
My eyes shall look downward
And my song shall be unsung
While you (I) stay on the old Va. (Ky) shore.

I inquired of a friend who specializes in the banjo and music from this era and he informed me that this was taken from My Darling Nelly Gray, B.R. Hanby (1856.) Notice he put the real words in parentheses.

Margaret has the measles, she got them a week ago today. She is at Olives yet and I guess is rather homesick. She will be 2 or3 weeks later getting out in the spring now.

As for the Van Horne girls there is two, Mae or May and Pearl. Jim went once with each. Sam is going with Pearl the youngest and best looking.

Our Mailman, Mr. Grimes upset on the Pounds hill some way Thursday and broke his wrist. His son drives on the route for he is unfortunate. Only a short time since he had foot taken off in a thrashing machine.

He closes by sending his love and best wishes.

41.　Martha - Jan. 15, 1903, Weston, W.Va.

She is still insecure unless it is her way of getting him to declare his love for her.

You don't know how I would like to sit behind the bells that is unstrung. But Frank you are just bluffing me, you don't mean what you said.

She is at church again and they are having a revival and all the

56

churches went together to have it.

Last night the church was crowded. I hope there will be great work done. For Weston is not very much of a church going place. Most of the people would rather go to these big dances and operas and this is an awful place for card playing. For such a small town.

I wish you could be here or at any other time, but you don't care to see me as I do you, anyway. So I presume there is not much use of me asking to come out before we move. We are going to tear up the first of March. They are going to move to New Martinsville W. Va. I guess it is handy Pitts or it is going in that direction at any rate. My time is out here the last of Mar. But they want me to go with them. I hardly have made up my mind yet. But I think I shall go for all I know now. For I would like to see the place. I would much rather go home first but I am afraid I cannot do that. But I will wait till the time comes to go. Maybe when I get on the train I will want to stay on and go to New Castle.

Even after his sweet poem of the last letter, she is not convinced that he wants to see her. She gives him a little tease at the end when she talks about staying on the train.

42. Frank - Jan. 18, 1903, Slippery Rock, Pa.

If my writing is poor and words misspelled in this epistle please lay the blame on the goal of the order of the [ooo] at Portersville Pa. I took my fist ride last night. You may have thought many times that I was queer but now you will think for sure that I am an Odd Fellow.

Frank made the symbol of three interlocked circles or triple links. They represented "Friendship, Love, and Truth. The Odd Fellows was a fraternal organization that originated in England in the eighteenth century. There are many theories on how the name was chosen. "Several theories aim to explain the etymological

57

background of the name Odd Fellows, often spelled Oddfellows in British English. In the 18th century United Kingdom, major trades were organized in guilds or other forms of syndicates, but smaller trades did not have equivalent social or financial security. One theory has it that odd fellows, people who exercised unusual miscellaneous odd trades, eventually joined together to form a larger group of odd fellows.[10]

If the sun were to shine much the sleighing would soon go. It is very poor in some places now. If you would like so much as you said you would to sit behind the bells.

I cannot see why you should wish to stay longer in W.Va. than you intended in the first place. Do you not think you are needed at home? If not can you not make yourself contented in New Castle? I think your sisters would welcome you.

If I am still as much of a friend as you say I am please write me a full outline of your plans for the future and especially your reason for thinking of staying in W.Va.

Your last letter makes me feel sad and has caused me to think of the letter I once gave you to read which I wished to forget. Hoping the sorrow was a mask over joy and that God will hasten your home coming is my prayer. I am what you wish me to be.

43.   Martha - Jan. 21, 1903, Weston, W.Va.

I include the entire letter because it is so heartfelt I cannot paraphrase it.

I have just come home from church and thought I would answer your message which was rec'd this morning. I have read it a great many times today. I feel very sorry my last letter has caused you to

---

[10] Wikipedia

be so sad. I cannot think what I could of said to make you so sad. You must of read it with a different meaning than I intended it for. I always like to make people cheerful and hope you are by this time.

You do not know how I would like to write and tell you of my home coming soon. But my sister insists so much on me going along with them to help move. And she has been so good to me that I hate to refuse. That is all the reason that I have for wanting to stay. I would much rather go to New Castle then I could see you once in a while. But I think while I am down here, I may as well go, I never expect to have the chance again and they say it is such a nice place. I would like very much to see it. And don't you think it would be wise for me to go? I think I shall only be gone a couple more months and when I go home <u>our</u> meeting will be a <u>greater</u> <u>one</u>.

I think of you just the same as when I left. But sometimes I have read your letters which has seemed to me as though you did not care to correspond to me. But I would think if you thought that, you would surely tell me, for I would not want to write if I thought you did not want to answer.

As for my future plans. I cannot write them. I have left them all with him who knoweth all things best. I am glad to know you can call yourself an Odd Fellow. I think it is all right to join them and hope you will find it a pleasure in going. I suppose you wear the three links.

Now Frank I hope you will gather enough from this epistle to cheer you. I cannot write all the thought I have. I would much rather go home than any place else if it was not for that one reason. I have not heard from home yet. Maybe they want me at home. I do not know. I wrote to them about going but they have not answered yet. I think I can be more able to tell you in the next letter.

Now I hope you will write very soon and hope you will be more cheerful. Your letter has caused me to feel unhappy all day and homesick if I must say and just that one reason that holds me here. I will close looking for an early reply. Bye Bye I am still you friend, Martha

CHAPTER 8

COUNTRY OR CITY

44.   Frank - Jan. 25, 1903, Slippery Rock, Pa.

He is now feeling better and is content with her decision because there is no other way out of it and he gives his consent. If she wants to see more of the country, she should do so.

In your observations which do you think; the people of the city or the country get the most value out of life?

I think he is testing her a little. This question is very important in their relationship over the next few months. Maybe Frank is feeling he is losing her to the city life.

Enough of all that and he changes the subject, well not really!

I got a new game board last week, crokinole carrom sets is the best I could get, it's a beauty. I did not need it very bad as I have no good players to help me but I will have it when I get one when you come home.

Although Frank called it crokinole carrom, that is not really the name. "The game of carrom is believed to have originated from

61

India. One carrom board with its surface made of glass is still available in one of the palaces in India. American carrom is a variant developed around 1890 in the United States by missionaries to Asia, who brought the game back with them. Concerned with young boys loitering around pool halls (where gambling was common), a Sunday school teacher altered the game for Western tastes. It is played on a board similar to crokinole but with pockets on the corners to sink your discs by flicking with your finger. It could look like a board game of billiards."[11]

There is not much time during the day that I am not thinking of you and when I quit writing I want it to be where you are handy enough to speak it to. My letters may not all be interesting yet they are written by one who loves you as he never loved before.

Frank is honest with her in declaring his love for her. He is longing for her to come home but realizes that cannot be at the present so he reminds her of his love for her.

We have rented Sam's farm for one year more. There is several around that would not be surprised if you and I should move in this spring.

I did not go to lodge last night as I thought it was too rough. I expect to wear the three links.

We have excellent sleighing now. Next Sunday is our Communion day. There is to be two or more nights of preaching this week. There have been some seven come forward for baptism at Harlensburg.
Hoping this letter may make you happy and again asking your prayers.

I am your Frank

---

[11]Wikipedia

45.   Martha - Jan. 29, 1903, Weston, W.Va.

Everyone is in a better mood now. Martha got a letter from home telling her it was okay to move with her sister because she wasn't needed there. She was glad for Frank's consent too. It will make the move much better since she may never have this chance again. To have the move paid for, and be earning a salary while there, is a good thing.

She has an interesting thought about Frank's question of the city or country life.

As to that question about the people of the city or the country gets most value of life. The city people has it more pleasant in social life than the country people have. While yet there is to much of the swell society in this town for its own good. Which there is no good in. I do not know that I can tell you which has the most value of life till I get your opinion. Although I have always been a little partial to city life. Not for it's society but for some reasons I cannot write now. It would take to long to write it all. But I do not know whether I am right or not in that.

You spoke of having good sleighing out there. While we have beautiful spring weather here it has been warm enough to be on the streets without a wrap.

The union meetings is still in progress yet. I have not missed very many nights in which I am organist part of the time. The church is crowded every night and five ministers. They have organized a young people Christian Band all the young Christians people is to join and to do all they can in this revival. There has been twenty or more joined which I hope will prove to be of good results.

I hear Sam is still attending dances. Oh if he just knew the results that comes from the ball room It is just like some people here. Good Christians they claim to be, they will go to church one evening and the next they will play for an opera or a Big Ball. I think it is simply awful. What do you think of that? Do you think it is right?

Martha is really showing her narrow views on the things of the world outside of her Christian circle. She is disgusted with ballroom dancing but in other letters she seems to be fine with square dancing. It probably has to do with the intimacy of the couples dancing. She puts Frank to the test asking his opinion.

I would like to see your new game board and play a game with you but there will come a time some day. I expect it would be like when we played checkers last winter. You would beat me.

46. Frank - Feb. 1, 1903, Slippery Rock, Pa.

He just got home from church and tells Martha some gossip.

Sam took Nora home again, he also took her home last Tues. night. Last fall he thought she was the kind of a girl to "Bull around with" but I guess she has changed for he denies all he said against her. Jim Vogan had his Miss Boyd of Princeton there.

I was at Butler last Thursday and Friday the rent is very high and still going higher. I would not care to live in that town unless I had steady work. I went to the theater Thurs. night and saw Harry Tracy, the murderer which the papers spoke of last fall. It was good of its kind but would soon get tired of them. A moral can be taken from the plays but to much is useless and perhaps degrading.

"Harry Tracy (23 October 1875 to August 1902) was an outlaw in the American Old West. His real name was Harry Severns. He is said to have run with Butch Cassidy and the Hole in the Wall Gang, and by the time he'd reached adulthood he was actively taking part in acts of robbery and theft. In all the criminal lore of the country there is no record equal to that of Harry Tracy for cold-blooded nerve, desperation and thirst for crime. Jesse James, compared with Tracy, is a Sunday school teacher."[12]

As to those who dance and still are Christians, I think if they can show that proof, "Thus says the Lord" they then have a right to glory in the worldly amusement. Hell on earth if they cannot find God's approval, then they had better be careful for He says "not all that sayeth Lord, Lord enter into the Kingdom of Heaven."

Frank tries to answer Martha's question about dancing. He must be careful not to upset her with an answer that is in favor of ballroom dancing. She is certainly against it as well as card playing or gambling. She is strict and legalistic from her religious background but is sincere in her love for the Lord. He is quoting from Matthew 7:21, "Not everyone who says to me, 'Lord, Lord,' will enter the kingdom of heaven, but the one who does the will of my Father who is in heaven."

He is going to dig coal next week or so and then plans to take a little vacation and see some country.

47.   Martha - Feb. 4, 1903, Weston, W.Va.

I have just came home from church where we had a fine meeting. There has been quite a number of conversions. I have not learned the number yet, but there is lots to be saved yet. I do not know how long they intend to continue them (the meetings). But I am sure a couple of weeks yet because it is just beginning to get interesting and souls being saved.

She always has an eye on what God is doing in His Kingdom.

She writes that she will be moving in a month, but she is glad she lived in Weston.

---

[12]Wikipedia

You spoke of going to see some country. I think there is nothing nicer than to travel some. I am not sorry I have spent the winter here. I think it is a good schooling for one to get out and see what the world is doing and how other people live. I expect when you go you won't write to me. You will find one better than I.

Again her insecurities are showing or is it an attempt to get Frank to visit her on his trip?

She states that she has written to her mother every week since she has been away. If she didn't she would keep her mother in despair. Again she mentions his trip.

When are you thinking of taking your trip? I hope you have a nice time when you get started (you had better come on to Weston).

48.   Frank - Feb. 8, 1903, Slippery Rock, Pa.

Small talk begins the letter saying there were not many in church due to stormy weather and snow.

Nora D. has another new fellow, Miller Reichert of Jacksville. I don't know where Sam will go now.

I have 190 lbs of coal out now, I want to dig some more this week and if I can get a reasonable amount out I will start on my trip about the 16 or 17... My supply of money is somewhat limited and I will have to confine my pleasure to suit that. I wish to spend a short time with my uncle Albert Brown in New C [New Castle]– and then I think I will go to Pittsburg and visit the Preachers Moore and Uptegraph. I have an uncle in Wellsville O one in Ohio opposite New Cumberland W.Va. one in Va. or W.Va. I don't know which yet and last but now least a Dear Friend with whom I hope to share my name in Weston. I would like to see all but can't say until later and perhaps not then if I find that "other girl" what the program will be. No one knows I am going and if God is

66

willing I hope to surprise several. If I should be permitted to see Weston you would not have much warning. Would I be welcome under such circumstances? If you have any special request to make I will try to grant it.

May God grant a rich blessing on Weston in her revival is my prayer.

49.   Martha - Feb. 11, 1903, Weston W. Va.

She did not go to church Sunday evening but is writing instead.

I am glad you still are in the notion of taking your trip. I hope you will be permitted to see Weston. I would like very much if you would let me know about what time you would come. But if it does not suit you to do that it will be all right with me I am sure you would be welcomed at any time and I would <u>glad</u> to see you.

The meetings are still in progress yet. There has been a great many happy conversions but I hope there will be still more. You would be surprised to go into a town where so few young men are Christians and old men as well. You have as many young men in your church at Zion that they have in all the churches of the town here. Of course there is some young men in our church that are good Christians and some that have just taken that step since this revival. But there needs to be more.

Martha is very involved in her church. She gives an evaluation of the Christianity of young men in her city compared to the ones at Frank's church, Zion Baptist. Does she see how her conclusion relates to the discussion about city life versus country life?

CHAPTER 9

TRIP SOUTH

50.   Frank - Feb. 15, 1903, Pittsburg, Pa.

Election Day - this letter is short and sweet.

I expect to go south the last of the week so "have your lamps trimmed and bright, be it morning, noon, or night." FVP

From the dates it looks like Frank was gone on his trip for ten days.

51.   Frank - Feb. 25, 1903, Slippery Rock, Pa

It was great that Frank got to visit Martha in Weston. There are no details of what they did for ten days but he gives a good description of his trip home from Weston.

I am going to write a few lines this eve until I get sleepy.
I got the train all night at Weston, changed cars at Fairmont for Wheeling. I then crossed the river and then I was at Bridgeport. I got a train on the Pennsylvania track for Wellsville where I arrived at about 5 pm.

I found my uncles all right. I went to East Liverpool that evening to see the sights. I left Wellsville at 12:20 pm Tuesday and got to New Castle about 4 pm. I enjoyed myself quite well at Wellsville. My uncle has two daughters and two sons the oldest girl 24 yrs is married but was at home for a while the next is 20 yrs and single. The boys are about 14 and 18 or near that.
I visited the potterys there and brought a dish home made there.

It is interesting that he comments that he bought a dish there. The Wellsville/East Liverpool, Ohio is very famous for pottery.

"East Liverpool's location along the Ohio River contributed to its growth over time, as did its local clay. Probably its most significant industry in the nineteenth century was pottery, originally made from nearby yellow clay. English immigrant James Bennett became the community's first successful pottery manufacturer in 1840, but it was not until the late 1800s that the town's reputation really emerged. Pottery manufacturing was a difficult operation originally. The entire product was constructed by hand, using primarily a potter's wheel. Once the potter completed a sufficient supply of pottery to sell, he would travel along the Ohio River or through the countryside selling or bartering his product to all interested parties."[13]

He adds the small talk of the week that he was gone.

There was another party at Vanhorns last Tuesday night several of the good people from around here was present but after all was there it was turned into a dance.

Oh no, I wonder what kind of dance this was?

Margaret got home last Saturday but Reno did not come I guess the weather was to severe for him. J.K. Vogan is in bed with the

---

[13]http://ohiohistorycentral.org/w/East_Liverpool,_Ohio

'gripe.'
Clara & Mont went to New Castle on Mon. or Tue. To get married
but as Mont got drunk they could not get their license.

Frank says he hopes she is not lonely and he thinks of her most of
the time.

52.   Martha - Mar. 1, 1903, Weston, W. Va.

I rec'd your welcome letter yesterday and was glad to know that
you had arrived safely home again. It has just seemed to me like a
dream that you was here this time last Sun. but I know you was
here. And I felt very lonely after you had gone. When even I look
over at the hospital I think of our walk through it. I presume you
are glad you are back to a good level country again.

It must have been a special time together that was needed for this
romance. Now he can understand about the places she would write
about such as the asylum.

You ought to of been here this week and seen the high water.   I
know you said you would like to see some high water. The water
was very high here yesterday. There was several families had to
move out down by the creek. I was down to see it and thought of
you while there. How I wished you could have been along.

This is an interesting little story that gives insight to the times.

I expect if you had of been here yesterday you would of laughed at
the gas and thought coal was all right. The gas went out and was
off all day till midnight. It was fun to see the people hustle a round
and hunt up wood to burn. The gas line has broke that was cause
of it.

Apparently they had telephones.

There was a man just got through telephoning up to me to come and help them sing in the Presbyterian Church tonight. Am I not getting popular though I am not sure whether I will go or not yet.

53.   Frank - Mar. 3, 1903, Slippery Rock, Pa.

This was such a sweet way to open his letter.

Since I wrote you last I have been sick or almost sick with the terrible disease called "The Blues" or something similar. I have not been bedfast except at night. I received your letter today and am somewhat better now. However I do not expect to thoroughly recover until your bright face is to be seen in the little Stone House on the hill.

Soon after leaving, I began to think as directed in Luke 14:28 to the end of chapter which please read.

I quote these verses, Luke 14: 28-35, from the King James Version which is what Bible version they would have been reading:

28 For which of you, intending to build a tower, sitteth not down first, and counteth the cost, whether he have sufficient to finish it?
29 Lest haply, after he hath laid the foundation, and is not able to finish it, all that behold it begin to mock him,
30 Saying, This man began to build, and was not able to finish.
31 Or what king, going to make war against another king, sitteth not down first, and consulteth whether he be able with ten thousand to meet him that cometh against him with twenty thousand?
32 Or else, while the other is yet a great way off, he sendeth an ambassage, and desireth conditions of peace.
33 So likewise, whosoever he be of you that forsaketh not all that he hath, he cannot be my disciple.
34 Salt is good: but if the salt have lost his savour, wherewith shall it be seasoned?

35 It is neither fit for the land, nor yet for the dunghill; but men cast it out. He that hath ears to hear, let him hear.

It is a beautiful thing to realize that Frank had the biblical knowledge to find verses that seem to apply to his life at the time. We see that in other letters as well. It seems that he is thinking about what kind of work he could do to plan ahead and make money.

I thought of several different occupations which are money making after you get promoted awhile but whether they are satisfactory all around I don't know. The one we spoke of short hand type of writing I am as yet in the dark about it as it would take all I have to take a course and if one is not extra the pay is like wise. However I might come out all OK.

Fathers horses run off last Sat at New Castle. He was taking some apples into a house and did not put the weight on the horses, a limb fell and startled them. They went slow enough for a while but soon got speedy. No damage was done except a few doz of eggs were smashed and everything covered with mud. They ran about two miles next East Brook when they were stopped going up a hill. Its his first run off and the horses are often left standing with out being tied but they are not doing much now so that made the difference.

I can picture the scene in my mind with his description.

I often think of our walks and talks together and while I would have been pleased to of seen the high waters, yet it would have had its disadvantage and I enjoyed myself as it was and feel thankful for the privilege which was you say may never come again.

PS. If you find fault to this letter remember I have the "Blues" FVP.

Frank had a wonderful visit with his sweetheart. Being together and walking and talking was important, but it made him a little homesick for her. He is determined to make a future for them.

CHAPTER 10

LONELY

54.   Martha - Mar. 7, 1903, Weston, W. Va

As I am very lonely this evening, I thought I would write you a few lines and try to cheer you up a little. I have been alone since Wed. morning except the three boys are here. Mr. Black's brother died. He lived in Brownsville Pa.   Mr. and Mrs. Black went to the funeral and they are not back yet. So that is the reason that I am alone.

I see it odd that she calls her sister and husband, "Mr. and Mrs. Black" and refers to her nephew as "the three boys," instead of my nephews. I wonder if the etiquette of the time required her to say Mr. and Mrs. Black because that is the way Frank would have referred to them.

She has thought of the Stone House many times and wishes she was there and said she hopes he is getting better too.

Cheer up Frank and don't let that disease get a hold of you. "Cast your burden on the Lord and he will sustain thee."

This is a quote from 1 Peter 5:7. Their spiritual care for each other

74

is very important in this long distance courtship.

I am unable to give you any good advice if I could I would gladly do so. You know what is best for you. Ask God's guidance in the matter and he will direct you into that which is the best for you. So do not worry and get wrinkles in your face over it.

Sun. I did not get this finished last night. Will do so now. Mr. and Mrs. Black arrived this morning at five o'clock. I was very glad to see them. I have not been quite so lowly today.

It has been raining very hard all day. I was at S.S. [Sunday School] I have just come home. I was at church at the Presbyterian Church this morning. They telephoned up last night. They would like if I would come down and play. So I went. I will turn out to be a Pres next. But I guess there is no danger.

I hope you will gather enough from this epistle to cheer you and hope you will be happier in your next letter. Life is short and we may as well make it as happy as we can. Now if I have said anything that will make you feel worse, tell me of it in your next letter for I would not do that for anything.

55.   Frank - Mar. 8, 1903, Slippery Rock, Pa.

When I receive your letter which I hope to receive tomorrow, I expect to find it slightly colored page being in such close contact with so much blue as my last letter contained. Since sending it I have been thinking that perhaps it was caused partly by me not placing enough confidence in God for direction.

They are seeking God in this relationship and now Frank has a wonderful idea that shows he is a man of God.

Since I came to my room this evening, I have been wondering if you would not each day read as it were with me, a chapter or more

75

in the New Testament beginning with Matthew so that by next Sabbath you would have read 7 chapters and read the 8th that day. I think that after careful reading of a chapter our minds will be in better shape for talking with God. If you think after you have prayerfully considered this you would like to read one or more chapters each day with me please let me know and any change you think necessary. It will greatly benefit me to know you are reading and praying each day <u>and it will do thee good</u>.

This section makes my heart swell with wonder at the thoughtfulness and gentleness of this man I only knew as a rugged old farmer man. He knew the power of scripture to keep their relationship on track and their hearts close. He depended on God.

I do not feel nearly so <u>blue</u> not, my principal thought was that perhaps we could not satisfactorily get settled for life's work, but I began to think that we have lived through greater difficulties we can with good reasoning get through this. I fear I often "strain at a gnat and swallow a camel."

He continues with small talk of the friends and parties, Clara finally got married. He got a music book but does not understand it very much and she will not understand what he writes her in shorthand.

The marks are short hand characters with the names of each. The characters are supposed to be written in one minute. This is part of the first lesson. Try to write the alphabet as that is what is called. I can read much better than I can write now." Frank included in this letter the alphabet in short hand.

I send best wishes to those who inquire of me and wish you rich blessings. I will not look for that <u>other one</u> until my hopes have died and you prove that you care not for me.

He ends this long letter with a quote, *"'Shakespeare says: Condemn the fault and not the actor of it.' Apply that always if you can in my case.*

56.   Martha - Mar, 16, 1903, Weston W.Va.

Martha is very busy getting ready to move. She spends a paragraph explaining her letter writing schedule.

To change the subject. It was a very nice gathering last Thurs eve. You heard me speak when you was here of Mr. Black joining that Lodge. The Masons. That lodge had a fine banquet last Thurs eve. I got an invitation to go.

So, I went it was held at the "Camden Hotel." All the men that was Masons was dressed in there uniforms. They had some speaking and a great big supper and we was seated at the table two hours.

So you may know what it would be like. I expect there was over ninety couples there. Of course there was some that was not coupled off. I had a very nice time and was glad I went.

She responds about Frank's idea to read the Bible together.

In regard to reading a chapter each day that is in the Bible, I think it is a very good suggestion. I am willing to do as you have bid for I know it will not hurt either one of us to read a chapter each day. It will do us good. I commenced where you said and have read the eight Chapters. Do you have any particular time for reading?

I was through the hospital again last Sat. There was several wanted to go through that had never been through so I went with them. Mr. Curtis took us through the same part that he did you and I.

She is again referring to the West Virginia Hospital for the Insane or the Asylum. She closes with the usual lengthy discourse of good byes.

57.   Frank - March 18, 1903, Slippery Rock, Pa.

I received my joy this evening as you say it was a day late in coming and I don't feel much like answering tonight as I am tired and sleepy. Spring is here or seems to be and one must make hay while the sun shines. I shall be pleased when you are at the Stone House which I see so often and am so far from it. I think after you are home a while you will think there is no place like home, even if it is on a farm. I have some fear of the city life and am learning to like the country very much. I suppose you will drop a frown at that.

Father is at Butler after a load of goods for Grandma. She is tired of the city as the rent is very high and it was getting very wicked as she thinks. She will live in Sam's house.

What has his grandmother seen that is so wicked in Butler?

Many are plowing around here. We have not got started yet but will try and make up lost time after we get some harness made, will have two teams then.

I do my reading in the Bible about 9 c'clock each evening. Have not missed any yet.

I suppose you signed your name in the register book on your last visit to the asylum.

Frank's sense of humor is delightful—or insulting?

58.   Martha - March 25, 1903, Weston, W Va.

You will half [sic] to excuse my lead pencil this time as my pen and ink is all packed up. So I just thought I would take a lead pencil and scribble you a few lines this eve. I would of wrote sooner but I thought I would wait and see about what time we would move. I am not just sure yet when we will start. But I think the last of this week or the first of next. We have things pretty well packed up now. We will be leaving Weston in a few short days. Now Frank I am not going to write much this time it will be short and S......I had a notion not to write till after we got moved but I changed my mind.

My S.S. teacher had a social for me last Mon eve. She had all the class and a few others invited in which we had a very nice time.

Well as it is getting late and I am as the old saying is tired. I will close for this time. I will try and write a longer letter the next time. This will be the last letter for Weston. My address is
New Martinsville
Wetzell Co,
Box 59 W.Va.

And I shall watch for a letter in that box or the time dated for I expect I will be lonesome and home sick after we move.
Remember me in your prayers.
Close as ever, Martha

I left in this closing because it is the first time she signed this way.

CHAPTER 11

MOVING

59.   Frank - Mar. 30, 1903, Slippery Rock Pa.

I have received 23 letters with the post mark of Weston W Va. And I am exceedingly glad you are on the road home, I wish you much happiness in you new stopping place. However you must pardon my selfishness as I hope you will get so homesick that you will only stay a few days instead of a few months.

He is happy she is on the road home. What is he thinking? She didn't say that, but it is wishful thinking on his part. But he continues with lovely words.

Spring is here, the birds are hunting nesting places. The flowers are tossing their sweet perfumes to the passerby. The earth is being clothed with that green garment which will soon wither and die.

Sam was at Pearl VanHornes last Sat night, he is changeable. He is going to work for Gilfillan above Harlansburg but it is doubtful if he stays long. Chester's social was very good, he has 20 or more pieces for his phonograph. I eat supper with Jimie McCracken. They got over $11.00 and they will paper the school house.

This is the one room school house was about a mile or so away from the farm. My mother attended there for eight years. She always said that the education was very good in this environment because if you didn't get it the first time, you would hear it again.

60.   Martha - April 5, 1903, New Martinsville W. Va.

We left Weston Wed. morning at half past eight. I hated to leave there. Seven of my associates were at the train to see me off. We had some fine times together. One of my girlfriends had a social for me the Friday eve. before I left which we had a fine time.

We have been in this town three days. I think it is a very nice place. We was at the hotel two days we came in our own house yesterday. I presume it is to times a larger place than Weston. I wish you could of seen this place instead of Weston. You would of seen more. They have a fine big courthouse here. Not like the one you and I went through at Weston. The river runs right along the town. I was down street Thurs eve. and saw one of the big steam boats coming in. It was going from here to Pitts. I hope I will be fortunate enough to get a boat ride before I leave. It is a great place for bicycles. The streets are just as level as the floor. We do not live very far from the railroad. I can see the trains pass from my room.

Sister has a lovely house here. It is in such a nice location. I can not just tell yet when I will be home. But it will be some time this summer. I have been away from home six months now. I am beginning to think I would like to see them all again and also <u>one</u> *who lives in Butler Co.*

Oh Martha, never make a promise you cannot keep. Frank remembers every word you say and write.

Tell Margaret and your mother that is a very good picture of them that is if they know you sent one to me. That would be just like you to use the camera when they did not want you to. Do you have a camera of your own? I think they are very nice you can have all kinds of pictures.

Is Minta still in New Castle? I have not heard from her for quite a while. It is really my fault. She wrote to me and I never ans yet. Are you still reading the Bible yet? I have read the book of Matthew. I suppose you will teach your class if they start up the school again.

61.   Frank - Apr. 8, 1903, Slippery Rock, Pa

Look how he starts this letter! A very poetic tale about his letter.

Carry me away at a rapid gait
To Wetzel Co.W. Va. State
In New Martinsville PO let me lie
And if Miss Martha Covert should happen in
Just hand me to her and see her grin.

He continues talking about the work on the farm and as he is working in the fields he can see the old Stone House. It makes him homesick for his sweetheart.

Does your folks know that you still write to the Butler Co. farmer? I have always managed to get your last few letters and our folks appear to think that we have quit. Do I do wrong to deceive them?

83

Just one week today since one of my cousins, Vincent Philips was standing by the R.R. Track in Beaver Falls and was struck and killed by one of the through trains from Pittsburg to Chicago. He was struck by the engine on the head and thrown about 50 feet however no bones were broken, he would have been 20 next May.

Little did I think when I saw him for a few hours in Pgh. [Pittsburgh] *last Feb. that I would help to carry his body to the grave. He was buried at Zion. Rev. Joe Updegraph preached the sermon, his text was in 1 Samuel 20th 3 latter part but truly as the Lord said.*

The verse says, "And David sware moreover, and said, Thy father certainly knoweth that I have found grace in thine eyes; and he saith, Let not Jonathan know this, lest he be grieved: but truly as the Lord liveth, and as thy soul liveth, there is but a step between me and death."

He continues with some small talk.

Sam likes his new place very much, he still goes to VanHornes. Jim Vogan has no regular place now he backed the envelope the way I began this letter and I guess it made her – Nancie Boyd, mad what would you of done if I had of backed yours that way?

I can only conclude that Jim Vogan put a small poem on the back of the envelope and Nancie didn't like it.

I have not missed a day in reading yet and I ask an especial interest in your prayers. I always pray for you. I sometimes feel as though you may grow to care but little for me but I hope your pleasant surroundings may not cause you to do that.

62.   Martha - Apr. 14, 1903, New Martinsville, W. Va.

84

I do not know whether my parents know we correspond yet or not. For I never say anything when I write to them. Yet I think they judge we do. It is all right to deceive your folks if you do not want them to know you correspond with me. I read your letter as if you would like to quit anyway. I do not know whether I read it with the same meaning you intended for or not but if you do think that, why tell me. I have never told you I did not care for you. I do not know why you should think so. I would like to be at home and save all this writing for I consider I am as tired of it as you. But am not quite ready to go home yet. Probably you will think I am a little hasty there. But I am not and do not read it that way.

They are still trying to sort out their relationship. The miles are making it difficult.

I think that Nannie Boyd treated Jim Vogan just right. It is well you did not put that on the envelope. For I think I would of treated you the same for that is no place for that kind of writing.

PS Now write soon for I am very lonesome. Sometimes when a letter does me lots of good and I hope there is nothing in this to make you feel bad. I did not get this sent off tonight as I expected to do for it was raining very hard and the post office is about a half mile from here. So it will still make it another day later. But I will try to do better after this.

63.   Frank - April. 16, 1903, Slippery Rock, Pa

I had begun to think that I had wrote something terrible in my last letter but I am glad my thoughts were untrue. Your letter was like sunshine on a dark nights day.

My parents would appreciate your being home very much, I know, as they often say I can't get a girl and that you are away in W.Va. as your no doubt tiring of such knowledge.

It sounds like his parents have doubts if Martha is going to come home. Maybe he should be in the market for a different girl.

Reno was to see Betsy last Sat night he did not stay as long as usual but went home in the small hours of the morning. Remember the time we came home at such time and got lost?

Harvest is over the corn is husked and most fed, the apples are getting scarcer and the grass has begun to show its self for to wither and die. About July 4 we will begin to cut our hay and wheat owing to the wet weather we have not got much more plowing done than when I wrote last.

At first I was puzzled by Frank reporting that harvest was over and corn is husked and most fed. This letter is dated April and in my recollection, corn is not ready for harvest until late July or August. So the corn that he is referring to is what had been picked last fall and put in the corn crib for drying and feeding over the winter. I remember the building full of dried corn with the husks on. My brother and I would go in that building and husk an ear and then pop the kernels out with our thumbs. I think what he means is most of the corn has already been fed to animals and now they can feed now on the spring grass.

What time do you read the chapter? On next sabbath is the 15 of Mark is that the same as you? I expect to go to New Castle to get some teeth pulled at Jackson on Sat a week.

I often dream of you and I think of you most of the time during the day and frequently dare to think of the time when we shall be no more two but one.

Give my regards to you sister and family and wishing you great joy. I can hope to be yours til death shall part.

He certainly is declaring his love for Martha and uses Biblical language in doing so, "For this reason a man shall leave his father and his mother, and be joined to his wife; and they shall become one flesh." Genesis 2.24

64.   Martha - April 21, 1903, New Martinsville, W. Va.

Yours which came to hand yesterday was gladly received as usual and with pleasure. I endeavor to answer this beautiful afternoon. I am sorry that my last letter was so dark and gloomy. But I guess I was likewise when I wrote it. I hope this letter will be more candid than the last. I sometimes think I would like to be at home. When I think of the time that is past and gone. I do not think I will forget the time we got lost. I do not know whether I will be at home for the fourth this year or not. Time will tell.

I am glad you revealed to me the fact that harvest is over. I have been in town so long I have forgot when harvest is yet I still know that you half to sow before you reap. And that is what I really meant when I mentioned it in my last letter.
Are you going to get your front teeth filled?

When you spoke of reading the 15 chapter of Mark did you mean on Sunday the 19th. If you did, I read the 16 of Mark that eve. So I am one chapter a head of you. I do my reading about nine or half past nine in the eve. Tonight I will read the second chapter of Luke. I have not missed any yet.

They are great example of a young couple trying to remain close through the word of God. It is important for them to keep each other accountable.

Where is Sam? Is he still working up by Harlensburg and who is he going with? No doubt you will be getting tired of these questions so I will not tarry you any longer this time.

65.   Frank - Apr. 26, 1903, Slippery Rock, Pa

During the past week we have been very busy sowing oats and as I am one of the church auditors I have been busy with that office at night.

I had the pleasure of hearing Rev. Timland preach today to the Odd Fellows and His text was in John 15:12-13.

These verses read, "This is my commandment, That ye love one another, as I have loved you. Greater love hath no man than this, that a man lay down his life for his friends." The Odd Fellows motto is Friendship, Truth and Love so the scripture was fitting for the group.

I have missed reading for two evenings but before this reaches you I will have been even with you.

Sam called a few minutes this evening, he says Minta is home but I judge she will be getting her name changed soon. We have got our new autoharp, it is a beauty but there is not been much music taken out of it yet.

The autoharp is a musical instrument in the chorded zither family. It features a series of chord bars attached to dampers, which, when pressed, mute all of the strings other than those that form the desired chord.[14]

I intended to get my teeth filled last Sat but it has been postponed for two weeks. It is 4 lower double teeth to be filled. I will keep my upper teeth as long as they are good to behave and when they get unruly they will come out.

Dental work was done in the early 1900's without using Novocaine. "... in 1905, German chemist Alfred Einhorn was able

---

[14]From Wikipedia "Autoharp"

to formulate a new local anesthetic called procraine [sic], which took away the discomfort patients had to endure previously. Heinrich Braun brought the material to the U.S. in 1907, marketing it under the trade name most people are familiar with today – Novocaine."[15]

"I will begin plowing for corn tomorrow we will plant about 18 acres.
Goodby for this time. Write as soon as convenient . Sabbath will be my most convenient day for writing for sometime.

---

[15]https://www.craigarmstrongdds.com/dental-technology/history-dentistry-1900-1955/

CHAPTER 12

LIFE IN NEW MARTINSVILLE

66.   Martha - May 5, 1903, New Martinsville, W. Va.

I felt very much disappointed last Monday a week when I rec'd no letter. Yet I know one working hard all day, they do not feel like writing when evening comes.

Even though he tells her how busy he is, Martha scolds him. She is so anxious to receive a letter from him no matter what he is doing.

I presume you are very busy now. I can imagine I see you going around the field plowing. You must expect to raise an abundance

of corn this year by the amount of acres you intend planting in.

Remember where we spent Decoration Day last year? This year we will be many miles a part.

Decoration Day is now called Memorial Day. It was called decoration because it was the tradition to decorate the graves of he fallen soldiers. There were no letters in May, 1902 so that means they were together last year for this holiday.

Is Minta at home yet? And is she really going to have her name changed or did you just add that is it. Does Victor go with her yet? Or do you know I wrote to her but I do not know whether she will get it or not. I directed it to Grantboro.

They have a Circle here called the Daisy Circle. I have been invited to attend Wednesday. If it is the Lords will I think I will attend. I do not like to go where they are all strangers but it is a good way to get acquainted.

A circle in church was primarily a group of women who got together to find ways to support their missionaries.

They are preparing to build a new Church here. Their church burned down here this spring and it was a fine church, but I guess this is still to be a finer one. We have church and all the meetings in the school building on the third story. There school is out here next Friday. Commencement is Friday evening, there is eleven to graduate.

This is a beautiful day it makes one feel like going out for stroll over these beautiful fields. I had quite a nice walk Sunday afternoon. There was one of my girlfriends that I have met. We are just neighbors. She came in and wanted me take a walk so she showed me the parts of the town that I not seen yet. It is a pretty large place."

It sounds like Martha is really getting integrated into her new life in New Martinsville.

67.　　Frank - May 6, 1903, Slippery Rock, Pa.

I have been plowing today and have enough to keep me busy for several days yet. What do you know of the country near New Martinsville? What is the principle crop? Also what businesses is principally cared for in town?

It sounds like Frank is trying to get to understand the town she is living in a little better by his questions. He must use his imagination to see her in all her activities.

I am getting another horse ready to drive single. I would like very much if you could cut your visit short and come home. I am very lonely these fine evenings. I think if your sister knew how much use you could be in Pa. she would not want you to stay.
I think Mint is home yet. I will add some more later as I am going or thinking of to a lecture at Harlensburg tomorrow night at the Presbyterian.

I expect to go via Vogans and perhaps take Mint that is if she will go. Charley McCracken and Amie Deare were married lately. I can play Rock a Baby on the autoharp. I don't learn very fast. If this is mailed at New Castle Friday, you may know that I am getting some teeth filled.

Nora Dambaugh on the church star dancers came last Sat to ch [church] meeting and confessed to having done something sinful. She didn't say what and she will try and not commit the same sin again.
Ps Thurs. I went to prayer meeting this evening. May Vogan was there and told me Mint was at Alice's helping to clean house. I think perhaps Alice is still getting fatter, been eating dried apples I guess.

May said Mint and Victor had quit but I could not believe her. I think these may be preacher happy within the next few months Have you any music students?

68.   Martha – May11,1903, New Martinsville, W.Va.

I presume you have went through the operation of having some teeth filled, as I see you mailed your letter in New Castle. I do not think there is very much fun in it. For I can sympathize with you. I suppose it is over with by this time in which you are not sorry.

I am getting acquainted with the good people of New Martinsville. There is some very nice friendly people here. I am unable to answer your question in regard to the place in which you spoke as I have not been here so very long and I have not inquired any about it. Probably I can tell you in some future time when I get to know the place better.

I have thought the same as you about these fine evenings. And have thought very much over the past but I want to get all out of this trip I possibly can and probably you had better find an other girl that is nearer that you can share these evenings with. I do not want you to feel lonesome and I know there is no use of me asking you to come here as it is a very busy season at present. I may not of showed my appreciation of you coming while I was in Weston but I did, if I did not show it at the present time.

Mrs. Black was taken very ill last night. But she is some better today. And it has left me very busy today and I wanted to get this letter off so I thought I would finish it if it was not written so good.

69.   Frank - May 13, 1903, Slippery Rock, Pa.

Your letter was welcomed today and I hope Mrs. Black is well by this time. I found out last Friday where your sister in N.C. [New Castle] lived. She has a nice place to stay.

93

I had 5 holes filled in 4 teeth. Jackson done it. It was not enough to kill you he was not an hour at it. I was agreeably surprised.

I saw Mint Sun evening, she says Victor and her have "quit" but I could not believe her. She is still working for Alice. I guess she will remain in the country for some time yet.

James Vogan has got a grand new buggy. Sam is going to trade his on a new one and Lewis Hunt is also getting a new one.

Chester is still going with Miss Douglas. I don't know where Lewis will go.
Margaret is still at home. Reno comes every two or three months and I guess writes a few times between.

It is very important for these young people to keep up with what is happening with their circle of friends. Frank surely wanted to keep Martha connected with home since she writes about all the new friends in West Virginia.

I do not have time to hunt another girl unless you think it best. I would not care to deceive her and be untrue to you. You no doubt remember our promise, in which was faithful until return. I often think of our lives as a story in which I long for the closing chapters. Sometimes I think perhaps my fortune may be like the 'Tramps Fortune' in the song. Remember such thoughts occasionally come into my mind but it is in noway my desire to see them fulfilled.

There we have it, they made a promise to one another to be faithful. Frank has full intentions to remain true to Martha. Isn't it ironic that he thinks of their lives as a story?

I dare say you often have such thoughts and there is many things which you cannot see clearly yet and I no doubt for the best that you cannot. I often think of the future and have some plans which I would like your approval but I cannot trust myself to write them. Do not worry about what they may be, for if it is God's will you may know them yet.

Do not think of my visiting W.Va. for a good while yet. I know I would enjoy myself but I wish to see such places as Niagara Falls and St Louis when I again have time to travel.

70.   Martha - May 18, 1903, New Martinsville, W.Va.

Mrs. Black is not very much better still. Saturday she took worse. The Dr. said she would half to be careful or it would turn to fever. But she is better this evening. I think she will get along all right. It seems to me the way you spoke that everybody out there is getting a new buggy. My, wont they feel big? It is all right. I like to see a nice rig.

I long for a buggy ride as we use to take of old. Why are you wishing for the closing chapters? They may come soon enough. We do not know what one day is going to bring forth. But yet I sometimes think there will come a time someday which will tell all.

When I spoke of some one else in my last letter, I thought perhaps you would like to enjoy life better than you are. I mean to have someone handier than I at the present time. And perhaps I was keeping you from it while I would not want to do that knowing I am many miles away. Yet I think of you the <u>same.</u>

Did Minta say anything about receiving a letter from me? I would like to see her very much. I had a letter from home last week which stated that Father was not very well again. I have not heard since. I intended to write home this evening too, but it is getting late and I guess I will wait till tomorrow.

CHAPTER 13

WORK ON THE FARM

71.   Frank - May 21, 1903, Slippery Rock, Pa.

I am tired and sleepy. I just came from prayer meeting there was not very many there yet the meeting was a good one. For even where two or three are gathered together in His name, they may have His blessing. I am expecting to spend Decoration at S.R.S.N. [Slippery Rock State Normal] again this year.

When Frank say S.R.S.N. I believe he referring to the college in Slippery Rock. Slippery Rock University opened its doors on March 26, 1889 as Slippery Rock State Normal School. It was a two year school educating teachers. In 1926 it became Slippery Rock State College and provided a four year degree. In 1960 and for the first time, it awarded undergraduate and graduate degrees in the liberal arts and in the professions and became Slippery Rock University.[16] Frank uses these initials often in his letters. It makes sense that there would be a celebration at this location.

I hope Mrs. Black is better by this time. I am expecting to dig coal tomorrow afternoon so if you don't get a letter again you may

---

[16]www.sru.edu/about/history

know that I have had some difficulty but I look for no harm as everything in the bank is OK.

72.   Martha - May 25, 1903, New Martinsville, W.Va.

I was glad to hear from you if it was short. I have been homesick today as I may as well say. I have had a longing for to see the "dear old time" and also <u>you.</u> Mrs. Black is getting a long fine. She is able to be up and a round again. I am glad she did not have the fever. I hope you have a nice time at Slippery Rock Saturday. I do not expect to go any where this year. I have not as yet heard of any thing going on here. So I will spend the day at home and be <u>good</u>. I presume you will have rain enough now to make plowing easier if it is raining as hard out there as it is here. We are having a storm here now. We had a very hard storm yesterday afternoon.

Are you still reading a chapter every evening before retiring? I read the thirteenth chapter of John this evening Is that where you are?

73.   Frank - May 28, 1903, Slippery Rock, Pa.

I have just come from prayer meeting again and though it is about 11 o'clock, I will endeavor to write a few lines as I am still on the top of the ground.

I was at Jacksville yesterday evening and did not get home until late on account of the storm. We have plenty of rain to do for a while now. We finished our last patch of corn yesterday.

Your letter makes me feel refreshed. The most interesting thing you wrote was that you was homesick. However I will not disappoint myself again by looking for you again till you arrive in New Castle. Remember, there will be more than one glad to see the prodigal return home..

I have missed some two or three evenings in reading but will make it up. I am glad you named the chapters you were reading.

Fri. I have been working corn this afternoon having a two horse work makes me lazy. But I suppose that is natural.

I will not go to S.R.S.N. [Slippery Rock State Normal] *or any place tomorrow as my horse has got a bruised heel, not bad, but she will be off work a few days. The other colt has not been worked for a bout a month owing to a sore shoulder. He is about well now and is spoiling for work.*

I am glad to see how well Frank takes care of his horses. He will skip entertainment for the sake of his horses.

I close and go feed the 8 pigs. We have about 200 chickens and 40 turkeys, always more to follow, and 3 old cats and 4 kittens."

CHAPTER 14

ARREST

74.   Martha - June 2, 1903, New Martinsville, W.Va.

I am getting along fine here. I am preparing to attend the convention if God is willing. We elected our delegates last night. There is five of us. They have put me on the programme too for music. I do not know how about that but I can and do the best I can.

I have met some very sociable people here and this is just a fine little town but last week I just thought that I could get on that train that passes our house any day and go to New Castle. I think if it had not of been that Mrs. Black was not very strong yet, I believe I would be in New Castle for I was very much discontented but your letter of yesterday was a great comfort to me. I would not want to leave Mrs. Black now, she is better but she is weak yet.

O Frank, I have something good on you which I hope is not true. What was you arrested for? I heard you were but I shall not believe it till you reveal it to me yourself. I did not learn why you were, so I shall be anxious till I hear from you. I have aways thought you honest and I hope you will be in this, if such is the case which I hope very strongly is all false.

What a surprise this must have been for Frank to read. Gossip travels fast. This seems very out of character for Frank!

Do you still drive 'Dick'? Is that the one that was hurt? I presume he would not know the old gatepost anymore as he use to. You must be kept very busy if you have all those things to feed you mentioned.

So funny she call the animals "those things." Sure sounds like a city girl to me. I think she must be referring to a gatepost at the Old Stone house where he probably tied old Dick when he visited her.

75.   Frank – June 4, 1903, Slippery Rock, Pa.

I was working in the corn field today and may work on the roads some tomorrow. Some of the roads are going to be fine for those who enjoy the pleasant rides with agreeable companions. I walk alone.

You need not think you are the only [one] *just because you are delegate to a convention. I also am a delegate to a S.S. Convention held at Beaver Falls. I am assistant superintendent and am to go in that place if I go. It is to be held in June 16 & 17. I think I may go.*

I once heard a man in New Castle say "if a young man was thinking of a wife he had better try to sell sewing machines. And after a few lessons in that business he would be glad that his life was not burdened with the cares of a woman."

While there is not much encouragement for me to get one yet I wish to learn and so when I am not busy I am going to sell some machines of which I send you a circular. We have used one for about 6 weeks and find them OK. I have sold two.

This is a very interesting bit of information. It is hard to say what kind of machine he had, most likely a treadle. There were electric machines in the early 1900's but probably rare out in the country. It seems Frank is always looking for a new way to make some money. He keeps trying new things.

He tells his sweetheart that he would like to see her the Fourth of July and then answers the big question.

As to my being arrested, I know nothing of it and have no idea what I have done that I might need be. I would like to know something more about it.

That is good news. Frank is innocent!

I do not drive Dick much now it was another one that was hurt but she is well now.

My cousin Charley P of N.C [New Castle] is here now he is about 16 years old and we have lots of excitement. Last night he took a frog to bed with him and when he thought I was asleep, he put it on my back but as I was not sound asleep he did not get all the fun he wanted. I suppose you may think it was foolishness but boys are young but once. He is greatly excited about ground hogs and has caught one.

It is so delightful to imagine the shenanigans of theses young boys.

Mother and Father have been married 26 years today.

This means my great grandparents, Jesse and Lizzie Patterson, were married May 28, 1877.

76.   Martha - June 8, 1903, New Martinsville, W.Va.

With pleasure I endeavor to answer your welcome letter which was rec'd Saturday evening and I read it in the high school building. The ladies aid society had an entertainment of moving pictures

Friday and Sat evenings that is one department of the church. Of course they had men to come here and give the entertainment and I was pianist. I read your letter before it commenced. I thought maybe I could play better, ha, ha. They made about one hundred and twenty five dollars the two evenings. The ladies get half of it. There was two of them just here and payed me for playing so I made a few dollars. Ha, ha.

You talked as if you was lonely. You do not know how I would like to take advantage of them good roads these fine evenings. I do not think it will be many more months till I am in the dear old house on the hills. I would certainly find it a pleasure to be in your company the Fourth. I am unable as yet to say for sure whether I will be at home or not for that day. It may be, time will tell.

I am glad you thought of starting in time but it does not happen to be sewing in a classes but I think those Separators are just fine. We have one at home it was not just the one you are selling. They save lots of labor and work. I hope you have success in selling themselves.

Then on to the big rumor, but she doesn't say much.

I am glad the report of arrest proved to be false.

CHAPTER 15

LONGING FOR MARTHA

77.   Frank – June 10, 1903, Slippery Rock, Pa.

I received your letter this afternoon and I enjoyed working corn better after that. The few dollars you got appeared to make you cheerful. I wish you lots of it.

I dreamdt [sic] *last night that we were in some town. I guess it was Pittsburg. We were happy as were going along the street, but it was only a dream to come true.*

I sent for another separator today, sold one to a Mrs. McClymonds who lives near Portersville. Margaret is at Olivers this week picking strawberries. I will go after her tomorrow. I read the eights of Acts tonight.

Thurs.
I was at Rose Point yesterday to get Dick new shoes. I stopped at Vogans as I came back. I thought there was mystery about the household and today I hear that Victor and Mint went to Youngstown in the afternoon and were married. J.K.V. would not give his consent. They went to his sisters and will be back Saturday.

It sounds like Martha's good friend got married. I wonder why they needed consent. It doesn't seem that there was much of a wedding party.

I rec'd another order for a separator today . I make about 40% there is a good many separators in the country.

I cannot get the connection between sewing machines and Separators unless it was a brand name like Singer.

78.   Martha - June 15, 1903, New Martinsville, W.Va.

I have four music lessons to give tomorrow. Besides some other business affairs to transact. So I am as busy as the mouse we chased around the room last night. We killed the poor innocent thing too. I guess we done as much jumping around as the mouse did. You just ought to have seen us after the poor thing. It was a sight to behold. Ha ha.

I am real glad to get a new cousin.

Sometimes it is difficult to interpret these hundred year old letters and this is such a case. I am not sure what she means about getting a new cousin. It is possible that Minta was her cousin and now she is adding Victor to the family.

When you write tell me if they have come back home and all the particulars and where they are going to live. I suppose they are happy but yours was but a dream.

I am glad that you are having success in the selling of those separators and wish you much of it.

I was glad you told me what chapter you read. We are just even. I read the thirteenth chapter of Acts tonight. So I will close for this time as I have lots of thoughts which cannot be written. It is eleven o'clock so I say Good night.

Hum, what are those thoughts Martha?

79.   Frank - June 18, 1903, Slippery Rock, Pa.

I came home from the convention this morning. I enclose you programs there was but few changes and the meetings were enjoyed by all. Miss Rowland & Nora Dambaugh & John Allison and myself were the representatives from our school. There are many things of usefulness which will be forgotten but a great many more that will be of some use as those live on who had the pleasure of being there.

I drove to New Castle and left my horse & buggy there. As I was coming out I drove past where your sister lives and saw your niece. I think she was surprised to see me.

I misinformed you about Minta & Victor. They were married in New Castle by the U.P. [United Presbyterian] preacher. They had engaged the Methodist minister but he was not at home. J.K. Vogan gave his consent before Squire Forbes. They are going now to Wilkensburg to live. I have not had the pleasure of speaking to them about their plans.

Wilkensburg is a suburb on the east side of Pittsburgh.

80.   Martha - June 29,1903, New Martinsville, W.Va.

We had just a fine convention. It was the first time I ever was at a convention and I hope it will not be the last. I enjoy them so much. There was five from here went. We started Wed. morning and went on the steam boat. We started at seven o'clock and got at McMechen, the place it was held at one o'clock. So we had just a fine ride on the boat. It was a treat for me never being on a boat before.

Martha had said after she moved there that she hoped to have a ride on a steamboat. Now her wish has come true. It is interesting that it is only 32 miles from New Martinsville to McMechen and today would be fifty minutes by car instead of the 6 hours on the boat.

On Wed. evening the McMechen people had a banquet for all the delegates and visitors in the town hall. So we marched from the church to the hall where the band greeted us with music and where there was fine refreshments. I think they had a fine program and everything was good. I will send you one there was lots of good things "said" of which as you say will be forgotten. The convention ended Thurs. evening.

The four of us stayed till Friday morning and then we went to Moundsville on the street cars and went through the W. Va. Penitentiary which I do not think I shall ever forget. There was 964 prisoners and they was all employed at some work. It was just remarkable to see how they half to work of which they could not do at all if they was out side of that.

"The West Virginia Penitentiary is a gothic-style prison located in Moundsville, West Virginia. Now withdrawn and retired from prison use, it operated from 1876 to 1995. Currently, the site is maintained as a tourist attraction and training facility ... In addition to construction, the inmates had other jobs to do in support of the prison. In the early 1900s some industries within the prison walls included a carpentry shop, a paint shop, a wagon shop, a stone yard, a brickyard, a blacksmith, a tailor, a bakery, and a hospital. At the same time, revenue from the prison farm and inmate labor helped the prison financially. It was virtually self-sufficient."[17]

This historical prison was interesting to read about but I am curious that tours were given while it was an active prison. My

---

[17]Wikipedia, "West Virginia Penitentiary"

grandmother got around during her time in West Virginia, from the Insane Asylum to the Penitentiary.

I had a letter from Minta. She is as happy as a bee now. They are going to board with his sisters till they get a house. Where are you going to spend the Fourth? I am sorry but I guess I cannot be at home that day for it would be impossible for me to get there now.

CHAPTER 16

THE INDIANS

81.   Frank – July 2, 1903, Slippery Rock, Pa.

I wish I could have been with you on your trip. But theres no need wishing now.
I was working corn yesterday and today. I had the pleasure of being at commencement at S.R.S.N. I secured a fine companion to bring home but as I could not make dates my hopes were built on nothing less than so much fun and foolishness.

I think I have found out where you got your information about my being arrested. I do not object to being talked about if the truth is told but I object to ---lies. The man doesn't have a mind of his own being ruled by his wife's relations. I am watching for more information and then ----- there will be a settlement.

Rev Howard Clouse a missionary and as a boy was raised near here is to preach at Zion next Sunday. He is from Oklahoma Territory. Works with the Indians."

In my pursuit of learning the history of the years in these letters, I looked up information about the Oklahoma Territory and particularly the Indians. I found that there was a book written about this titled, "And Still the Waters Run: The Betrayal of the Five Civilized Tribes" by Angie Debo (1940). I found it on-line for $299.36, but did not buy it. The book, "detailed how the allotment policy of the Dawes Commission and the Curtis Act of 1898 was systematically manipulated to deprive the Native Americans of their lands and resources."[18] As I read about this I realized that the Curtis Act took place five years prior to Frank attending a service where Rev. Clouse speaks about working with the Indians. I must say, it may have been a very interesting sermon. I wonder what the Eastern states were hearing, politically speaking, about what was happening "Out West."

82.   Martha - July 6,1903, New Martinsville, W.Va.

There was some parts of your letter that I could not clearly understand but I will leave it till I see you then you can explain.

I was not thinking any more about your arrest. I took for granted it was all false and let it drop at that. I will also tell you who told me when I get the privilege to see you which I hope to have before many more days.

My brother Charlie & wife and Harry spend the fourth with us. Harry left yesterday afternoon and Charlie and wife this morning it made me a little home sick when they left but when your letter came it cheered me up a little.

83.   Frank - July 9, 1903, Slippery Rock, Pa.

The Fourth was very quiet here I was at no big gathering just stayed at home. Jim Vogans horse kicked him a few times & smashed his new buggy up pretty good on the morning of the fifth. He had his girl and was about home with her, she was not hurt. Sam & Jim still goes to VanHornes.

---

[18]Wikipedia, "History of Oklahoma"

Whenever you come home if you have not better plan for yourself I would be pleased to meet you at the station.

Hoping you are well. I close and go to work. We have our wheat in sheaves and rye cut but not all tied in sheaves. I read the 9 of Romans tonight.

CHAPTER 17

PLANNING A VISIT HOME

84.   Martha - July 13, 1903, New Martinsville, W.Va.

It is not clear whether she is talking about going home permanently or just for a visit.

I had thought of going home the last of this month and I think I will if nothing happens. You spoke of meeting me at the station. I would be pleased to of had you meet me.

It was complicated for them to make arrangements for transportation to and from New Castle as well as other places. Martha goes on for another paragraph talking about the possibilities. Not only do we have the ability to pick up the phone or text someone for a ride, our mode of transportation is easy and fast.

I thought you was going to have a big time the fourth but your letter does not speak that way. I read the 13th of Romans tonight. I guess we are both at the same place.

85.   Frank - July 15, 1903, Slippery Rock, Pa.

Your letter came today and I was pleased to know that you are coming home. I hope your plans may not needlessly be prolonged. As soon as convenient I would be pleased to meet you. I will try and await your coming as best I can it has been a long time since we were together.

Martha left for West Virginia October 6, 1902. After four months, Frank went to Weston to visit her for a few days. So now it has been about six months since they have seen one another. Frank is anxious to see his sweetheart.

Miss Weimer is here now. I wish you could of met her. There is to be a lawn fete or fake in honor of her and Dedie Kelly Friday eve. at Dambaugh. Miss W. leaves Saturday.

It is fete (fet) not fake and it is a word we don't use much today. It means a large elaborate party, often outdoors.

We are busy with our hay now. Harvest will soon be over. Rem "When the Harvest days are over Jesse Dear."

These words must have been from a song they knew, however I could not find what it was.

86.   Martha - July 20, 1903, New Martinsville, W.Va.

I have been on the sick list for over a week but I am better now. I was afraid it was the fever but I am awful glad it was not. There is so much of it around here.

Martha refers to the fever. A newspaper article, from a town about 50 miles south, written several years earlier said that physicians differ in their opinion as to what kind of fever it is (there had been a severe breakout of many people). Some say Typhoid and some say a mild kind of yellow fever. Either one would be dreadful to acquire.

I do not know when I will start home. I can not go till Mr. Black comes, he will go as far as Pitts with me. He is out in the oil field now. But I am sure it will be a week or more yet before I will be home.

It has been a week since her letter trying to make plans for her arrival and now she continues for another paragraph trying to make plans for Frank to come and ride her home. She says she doesn't want to ask too much of him, but we can see he cannot wait to see her.

I got my pictures taken and they are peach I have one for you if you want it. I had thought of sending it but I guess I will wait now till I see you or I mean till I come home.

87.   Frank - July 22, 1903, Slippery Rock, Pa.

I am delighted to know that you will be home after your extended visit. I count it a pleasure to be permitted to meet you at N.C. [New Castle] and bring the wanderer back to the fold. It will soon be ten months since I have been at or past the Stone House. I am no doubt a stranger there.

Does Frank really think she is coming home to stay? Bringing the wanderer back into the fold sure sounds like he thinks she coming home for good. Oh, but we will see. He continues on with a paragraph about the plans to pick her up.

It is just 5 month tomorrow morning since I left the one I loved & I hope that ere 5 days pass you may be on your way home.

I notice they never say much about love and do not sign the letters, "With love," or something like that. It is refreshing to see that he calls her "the one I loved".

I am pleased to know that I am at last to get one of your pictures. The one I have answers the purpose very well but a later one will no doubt be good to help catch rats.

What in the world could he possibly mean when referring to her picture this way? Oh, Frank, I think you may have made a mistake!

Jim Vogan got his buggy kicked badly again last Friday evening as he was going to VanHornes. I guess he is going to quit driving the sorrel.

Sorrel is the description of a horse that is a light bright chestnut color often with a mane and tail of lighter color.

The lawn fete was very good considering the rain which spoiled part of the programme. On account of the wet weather we have not got much of our hay in yet. We have put up 11 loads.

88.   Martha - July 27,1903, New Martinsville, W.Va.

I am real glad to know that you can take the wanderer back to the fold.

She makes this comment and then as in previous letters has another

115

paragraph trying to plan her arrival and transport from New Castle to the Stone House. She tells him that Mr. Black is going part of the way.

I am getting very anxious to go now and if nothing happens I will go next week.

Now for her comments about catching rats with her picture.

If my other picture answers the purpose for to catch rats, probably I had better give this one away for I know you could not catch a rat with it, for it would scare them all away.

She seemed to take it all in fun.

89.   Frank - July 29, 1903, Slippery Rock, Pa.

I received your epistle today & had been hoping that you would have been home much sooner but I am pleased that I must wait no longer than Aug 9. It will be a long week and if you can come sooner let me know Sat. excepted unless you come with Father in the wagon.

I must of made an awful blunder in my last epistle since you understood that I said your photo is to catch rats. I hope you can forgive me. I meant it not, I say no more or I make it worse.

If you could of seen me Sat and Sunday you would of desired my picture very much. One of my teeth was troubling me and my face was exceeding fleshy it is better now.

We have all the hay on our own place up. Had some 32 loads all no 1. we have several acres on Sams place to mow yet. It is no 3 or 4 or more. However there is some is pretty good.

This was a mystery to me but it seems to be some method of

grading the quality or amount of the hay.

Next Sabbath is our Communion day. I expect we will have our extra good sermon as our pastor has finished his vacation.

I expect to mail this at Rose Point tomorrow. I am going to take a colt to the shop for shoes. Hoping this is my Farewell letter to W.Va. For many months and that it may be better than the last one. Give my regards to you Master and Mistress and children and write soon.

As ever yours, Frank 2 Tim 4-7

This verse in 2 Timothy 4:7 says, "Think over what I say, for the Lord will give you understanding in everything." What message is he trying to give to Martha? He seems to know his Bible pretty well to be able to pull up a verse to quote something meaningful to their situation. Um, could I do that? This is another evidence that he was familiar with his Bible.

90.	Martha - Aug 5, 1903, New Martinsville, W.Va.

I have been in hopes of going this week but the way things looks I am afraid I will not get off yet. I am still in hopes. Mr. Black was going part of the way with me and he was called out to his work so if he gets the tools out he will be in and I will be ready to go, for I am very anxious to go and can hardly wait till the times comes.

These plans have been going on since July 13 and are still uncertain. I can imagine that Frank is getting pretty anxious.

And do not look for another letter from me till I am in New Castle and I will write when to come in. That is if I go the last of this month or first of next and if I should be unable to get off then I will write to you.

117

CHAPTER 18

HOME FOR A WHILE

91.   Martha - Aug 13, 1903, New Castle, Pa.

Well Frank, what do you think? I am in N.C.[New Castle] at last, arrived last evening. Would be pleased to see you next Sunday. Come in Sunday morning and be here for dinner and then we will drive out home in the afternoon if that will suit you. Hoping to see you soon. Will close. I will look for you soon.

They are finally together! Now they can again build their relationship in person. Whether she is in New Castle or Rose Point, it is better than West Virginia. There is a short note below in September but then none until she goes to Pittsburgh.

92.   Martha - Sept 28, 1903, New Castle, Pa.

I suppose you are beginning to think I have forgot to write to you since I have come to town. But I have not, I thought I would wait till I could tell you when I would be home. I will go home either today or tomorrow. I want to go out with Jimmie C. and he did not know which day he would be in.

So I will just half to watch for him for I do not want to miss him. I suppose if I do I will half to stay in here, But I want to get home so I will watch.

I would be glad to see you Wed. evening if that will suit you and if not why you will half to set the evening and come when you can. I will be glad to see you any time.

I am invited to a party if I stay in tonight. What do you think of that? But I will not stay for that if Jimmie comes in. Well I guess that will be all till I see you.

They were in their early twenties and parties were as important then as young people getting together is today. But she certainly would not miss her ride back home to go to a party.

93.   Martha - Nov 24, 1903, Pittsburg, Pa.

She has moved to Pittsburgh for a few weeks with her sister Birdie and husband Herman Sachs in a suburb called Lawrenceville.

They was looking a little for me yet they thought I may not come till Tuesday so I surprised them some. I found them all well and as busy as ever in the shop. I expect you will not know me when I come home. I will be so fleshy eating so much meat.

I wonder if the shop would be grocery shop or a butcher shop at the time because she talks about eating so much meat.

Well did you get home all right? You had better explain to me when you write why you changed your mind so quick and staid [sic] in N.C. [New Castle] all night. I was sorry I did not get to see you some that morning but you ought not of told me a 'fib'.

For some reason she did not get to see him before she left for Pittsburgh. But she gets over it quickly and changes the subject.

119

I am writing and eating an apple don't you wish you had a bite ----

Herman and I was down town this afternoon and purchased a piano. It is to be brought here tomorrow. I do not know how Bird will like it but I tried to do the best I could. It cost $450. They are going to swing it in one of them front windows tomorrow.

It is interesting to see the price of a piano in the early 1900's. I wonder if when she says, "swing it in one of those front windows" she means hoist it up to the window in the apartment above.

94.   Frank – Nov. 29, 1903, Slippery Rock, Pa.

Your welcomed letter Friday (Thursday being Thanksgiving no mail came) and on Friday night I was at a party at James Book's and did not have time to write then and I think you may realize how I have felt when you went in W. Va. but of course you will not miss me as you will be enjoying your self being away from home. You had better get a pair of large new shoes as your toes will no doubt get sore after living so high.

It sounds like a little sarcasm here. I never heard of the expression "your toes will no doubt get sore after living so high." Martha is away from home more than Frank, so is he a little jealous about that? Is he worried that she is having such a good time she will not miss him?

Frank gives the explanation Martha demanded from him about staying in New Castle.

I intended to give you a surprise last Monday morning but it came near being the other way. I knew I would not be expected home until Mon. A.M. So I thought I would try and sell some more poultry and call at Zieglers on Superior St. Was not thinking of you leaving so soon and I was longer down town than I expected, so I think I was well punished for keeping the knowledge from you.

I went <u>up</u> to <u>Munnells</u> and got a share of the bed with Lee Carlton. He works for Munnell. I got home OK and it was a great deal nicer than going home after night by myself.

Here is what I think the story is about. Frank told Martha he was going home from New Castle on Sunday evening but planned to surprise her Monday morning with a visit to say good bye. He stayed in town at Munnell's but on Monday morning he went to sell his poultry and he missed her. His mistake was trying to surprise her Monday morning. He not only missed saying good bye before she left for Pittsburgh, he had to explain fibbing to her.

He changes the subject back to the party.

Finch was the principal game at Books. There was some music by McCrakens. They have just got a new piano. There was no kissing games that I saw.

I was at Rose Point yesterday and got my horse sharp shod so as soon as you are ready to come back let the roads be splashy or icy I will endeavor to go after you.

"Being sharp shod meant that the draft horses were outfitted with shoes that carried calks at the heels and at the toe. The calks' purpose, of course, was to provide traction for slippery surfaces–especially ice and frozen ground–because a bare foot or a regular plate wouldn't allow the horse to get the traction he needed."[19]

I hope you will be permitted to visit the many interesting places in the city. Go while you have a chance.

After telling her she is living so high he says to "go while you have a chance" and even underlines it. Even though he says she is "living so high" he still wants her to see what she can because his underlying thought may be, you might not get another chance after you become a farmer's wife.

Apples are to [sic] cheap to want your bites but I had a better supper than you had. I had 'thickened milk'. I am going to make some ice cream some time soon too.

I wasn't sure what thickened milk is, so I added a recipe:
"Grew up up on this hot cereal. Real good especially with just a touch of cinnamon sugar and/or molasses. Ingredients: 4 cups 2% milk, 1 tsp vanilla, 1 cup all-purpose flour, 1 egg. Directions: Heat the milk in a sauce pan with the vanilla. In a bowl mix the flour and egg with a fork. It will be crumbly. When the milk is scalding add the flour mixture to the milk and whisk. Turn the heat down to med-low. Continue to whisk till thickened. Finished product will be lumpy.

Serve hot with optional toppings: sugar, cinnamon, molasses, or honey."[20]

While you are reading this I expect to be under the ground as I shall dig coal Tuesday.

---

[19]thehorse.com
[20]Recipes.sparkpeople.com

There was not very many at church today. The roads are in fine condition and a little more snow would make good sledding.

95.   Martha - Dec 3, 1903, Pittsburg, Pa.

I will endeavor to answer your welcome letter this morning. I had begun to think you had never got home when you was so long about writing. But of course you was having such a good time you did not think about me and that was right. I do not blame you for if I had of been along at the party I would of just made you "feel bad" anyway. So I am real glad you had a nice time.

Martha is having such a hard time believing that Frank cares for her. I think at the word "party" all kinds of things go through her mind, especially when he mentions kissing games. But a party is fine if she is going to one.

Frank, you will have to excuse my lead pencil this time as Herman has the ink in the shop so I thought a lead pencil would answer the same purpose.

O, I must tell you the surprise we had on Birdie and she was so surprised she did not know what to do. We had a surprise party for her last night. Herman and I have been working for it ever since I came in and she knew nothing of it. So to get her away from the house till all the ladies came, there was one of the ladies came and invited us all up to her house that evening, so of course we went and when we got there the house was all dark and no one at home and she did not know what to make of that. So Herman told her we should just come home and have some music. So while we went to this ladies house they all came and was in the parlor in the dark. As soon as we come home we came up the stair to have some music and just as she got to the door Herman turned on the light. She did not know what to do. And we served a fine supper. She could not see where we got all that of course it was brought in. He had ordered everything and it was certainly nice and every thing worked so nice. She isn't over it yet this morning she is so beat.

To change the subject, you very near came surprising your self Monday morning instead of me that is the way untruths generally work. And you know all the time you was not going home and you telling me all the time you was going home that night.

Martha comes back to the issue that happened before she left New Castle. It sounds like she was very hurt by his actions and chastises him again for not telling the truth. She doesn't take into consideration that he was planning to surprise her just like they had to tell a fib to surprise Birdie.

I intended to go out and see Minta today But I am not feeling very well and I do not know whether I shall or not this afternoon.

Minta had moved to Wilkensburg which was only a few miles from where she staying now.

I do not know when I will be home I wanted to go next week but they will not hear to it. But if I do not get better I will go. I do not know whether I am living to high or not. Probably that is the cause of it. If I should go it will be the last of the week and I will write from New Castle when to come in after me.

96.   Frank - Dec. 4, 1903, Slippery Rock, Pa.

This envelope had a poem printed on the front left side that read:

The Liquor Bar
****

A bar to heaven, a door to hell,
Whoever named it, named it well.
A bar to manliness and wealth,
A door to want and broken health.

A bar to honor, pride, and fame,
A door to sorrow, sin and shame.
A bar to hope, a bar to prayer,
A door to darkness and despair.

A bar to honored useful life,
A door to brawling senseless strife.
A bar to all that's true and brave,
A door to every drunkard's grave.

A bar to joys that home imparts,
A door to tears and broken hearts.
A bar to heaven, a door to hell
Whoever named it, named it well.
******

Temperance Series, No. 1. 30c per 100
Address ADVOCATE Office, Fort Scott, Kans.

I was sorry to learn you were not well and I hope you may be better by this time. I would be pleased to hear from you Mon. if possible. There is so much sickness at Butler and other places that I will not be contented until I hear you are better and will be more happy when are home.

The roads are fine for traveling although a little icy. I was at R.P. [Rose Point] again today. We have a good load for tomorrow consisting of butter, chickens, lard, ribs & backbone of 3 pigs and over 100# sausage, two calves, apples & buttermilk, etc.

The next day, December 6, would be a Saturday and he describes a "good load" to take to the market. It would be interesting to know more about the market. The pigs had been slaughtered but was he selling live chickens and two live calves?

There was a dance at Rob Gordan's last night. There 35 or 40 there among those present was Sam, Clarence and Jim. Jim goes with Gertrude Dean now. There is to be a party at Jess Jones next Friday night. I wish you could be present.

I have to wonder what kind of dance this is. Back in a letter in January Martha makes her opinion very clear that she did not approve of dancing.

I have just got some new envelopes. I send one hoping someone may read the writing and be benefitted there-by. I expect to go to Harlansburg to church Sabbath. Do you go to any church? Have you been to any of the parks? Heinz Pickle Factory? Or any interesting place?

The Heinz factory (noted for Heinz Ketchup) was only a few miles from where Martha was staying and was a very popular tourist attraction, even when I was a little girl.

PS. Try and give me some idea where to meet you any day will do.

Why did you not stamp your letter? I read the 17 of Rev. [Revelation] *tonight.*

They are almost finished reading the New Testament together.

97.   Martha - Dec 7, 1903, Pittsburg, Pa.

I do not want you to worry a bout me. I am better now and I think I will continue this at least I hope so.

I told you in my last letter that I was expecting to go to see Minta that afternoon. But I was not able to go so I am expecting to go this afternoon. She will begin to think I am not coming.

I have not been to see very much of the city since I came in. It seems they are so busy here in shop that I do not want to take there [sic] *time.*

Last Sun morning a week ago we went to the Lutheran Church. That is the church they belong to and last night 'The Elks' that is lodge, held there memorial services in the Grand Opera House. We were there it was very nice. It was very sad. It was held for the members that had died this last year. And I was at the theater one night. I am getting good am I not.

I found a most interesting bit of historical information about the Grand Opera House in "The Pittsburg Post" July 26, 1903. The article is "Moving a Great Brick Building." This opera house was moved twenty feet as part of improving the downtown area of Pittsburgh. Apparently the move was successful because Martha attended a function there on December 6, 1903. It seems amazing that they were able to accomplish such an undertaking in the early 1900's

You are surely getting good when you are going to dances. You did not say you was there but I just took from your letter that you were.

127

It seems they are having all the parties when I am away. I would certainly enjoy being home for the party Fri. eve but I am afraid it will be impossible. For Mame wanted me to stay with her a few days on my way home. I think if nothing prevents me I will start for New Castle Thurs. or Fri. but I can not say for sure. If I should I will drop you a line.

98.   Martha - Dec 10, 1903, Pittsburg, Pa.

As I did not rec'd no letter from you to day I will drop you a few lines to tell you can meet me in N.C. [New Castle] Sunday any time you wish. Or if you should not get this Sat. why come in after me when you do rec'd it. But I think you will get this Saturday so you can come after me Sunday. I hope so any way.

CHAPTER 19

SETTLING BACK IN NEW MARTINSVILLE

Timeline review – Martha went to Weston, West Virginia in October, 1902, and from there she moved to New Martinsville, West Virginia in April, 1903. She had been in West Virginia for about ten months so she went home to New Castle and the Stone House in Pennsylvania in August, 1903. She remained in Pennsylvania until February, 1904 when she moved back to New Martinsville.

During that time in Pennsylvania, she stayed in Pittsburgh for a couple weeks.

Frank and Martha were together on and off for about six months. They were able to look each other in the eyes, hold hands, and maybe a sweet caress. They would talk about all those things that they didn't write down. There would be parties and games, sleighing fun and laughter, and many church functions over the holidays. I am sure that their relationship needed this because of the lengthy separations and with more to come. They would be separated again for almost seven months. The letters continue from New Martinsville, West Virginia.

99.   Martha - Feb. 26, 1904, New Martinsville, W. Va.

129

I will endeavor to write you a few lines to let you know we arrived here all safely. We didn't have a bit of bother. We left New Castle on the five o'clock train in the morning and was in Pittsburg at eight. Our train was just there for Wheeling but the train was delayed on the account of a wreck so we missed our train in Wheeling for New Martinsville and we had to wait there three hours and a half so we got here at five o'clock. We would of got here at one if we hadn't of missed that train. Laura was kind of looking for us of course she was't expecting mother. She was so surprised she didn't know hardly what she was doing. We found them all well.

This is a lovely two and a half hour drive today but took them twelve hours in 1904. It is wonderful that her mother, Adaline [sic] Covert was able to travel with Martha for a visit. It will give the ladies some fun time together.

O, yes that strap on my trunk didn't stay with me very long. Some person had the cheek to take it. I think if was taken of before it ever left N.C. For I would often see them changing it in one train to the other but I didn't think it was mine. I was looking for the strap. I guess some person thought they needed it worse than I did. It was well & had the rope on.

I never heard of the expression of "the cheek" and thought I misread it but I looked it up. It was correct but the word cheek is not used so much in this way anymore. It can mean nerve, gall, or hutzpa.

100.   Frank - Feb. 29, 1904, Slippery Rock, Pa.

The next day after I gave you good bye I was to see grandma and as I came of [sic] the porch and as I was leaving I had a misfortune and I didn't light on my head anyway. I bear the marks yet, but don't mention it.

As soon as I got home I found a letter waiting with an invitation to attend the Leap Year Party tonight. It was from Josephine Harlan. I promised to go but there was a thunderstorm this evening like the ones in summer and it has been raining from about 6 until now 9:30 and as I don't go to church when it is rough I did not feel like going to the party. I will go up with my excuse tomorrow.

It is so nice to see how Frank reasoned on this matter. It is rarely considered these days. If the weather is too bad to make it to church then it is too bad to go a party, or shopping or a football game or any other form of entertainment.

Billy is here tonight and Bert is at your place he started about 4 o'clock did not have any supper this makes the 3 times for him in the first week. I think I could take many a lesson from him when you come back and if Mae is as much in love with him as he with her you will likely have to come home sooner than you expected to play the wedding march.

You can tell MaMa to get ready to give her consent for Bert told Papa the other day if he ever found a girl that suited him he wouldn't go very long before he knew what the answer was. He would like to settle down. He enjoyed himself at the S.H. [Stone House] very much last Thurs eve. I gave him Polly to ride he put her in the stable.

Oh how sweet, we can see love is in the air with Martha's sister Mae, and her beau, Bert. Frank is very interested in this because he has the same thing in mind.

I have just been reading some of your letters that you wrote when you first went to N.M. I hope what few we write may have a different ring to them for I think we understand each other better now than then.

There is a new tone to this letter. It is important that they had some time together. He is now signing his letter "Your Hubby," Frank. Previously his letters were signed in the usual way, "As Ever," "I am faithfully yours," and occasionally, "Your farmer friend."

101.   Martha - Mar 3, 1904, New Martinsville. W.Va.

We had a thunderstorm here this morning and it rained awful hard. The water is standing in pools and is still raining hard. Probably I will get to see a flood yet they say the river is raising but I do not think it will be like the last one was.

It didn't take Martha long to get back into her church work. She said that she was at the church on three different occasions this week and the pastor came to visit her and her mother.

Everybody was glad to see me back or at least they seemed to. There was one old lady at prayer meeting last night that I thought was gong to eat me up. She called me "Dear" and everything nice. She was so glad to see me back.

Mother seems to be enjoying herself. Her and I took a walk over some of the town yesterday. It was such a nice day. She is going out to see my brothers next Sunday and stay a week with them.

It is nice for Martha's mother, Adaline, to see that her daughter is doing so well and the people in West Virginia really care for her. Martha was only twenty-two years old, so I am sure that it was pleasing for her to see her little girl has grown up to a fine young woman.

The interest in Bert and Mae continues.

I think Bert and Mae must be pretty sick. Mother said she thought they were not obeying the rules of the house to be up so early in the morning. You can tell Mae that when you see her and see what she says.

Did they go to the party? Mae said she got a bid to go. It was to bad it was such a disagreeable evening. I presume there would not many go. I was glad you got an invitation. It was to bad you didn't get going of course I mean on the account of the weather.

I didn't get this sent off this morning so I will finish now. I just came from giving a music lesson and Mall just came home and said that there was going to be a worse flood than before and every body is hauling there buggies up here on this street and there is four or five hearses setting out here too. So now if you should not hear from me for a week don't be scared. You can answer right away mebby [sic] the rail road won't have to stop running. But don't be scared if you should not hear from me within a week, but I will answer when you write if the train is going.

If you go over to see our folks you can tell them not to be scared we will be alright. It will half to be a pretty bad flood if it gets up here. They are looking for the flood about tomorrow or Saturday.

102. Frank - March 6, 1904, Slippery Rock, Pa.

Frank starts this letter with a report on the weather and all his activities, parties and card games, and of course he reports latest on Mae and Bert.

The evening is very rough, it is raining and there is no church handy so I am at home this evening. Had it of been nice I would of taken mother to Mt. Union tonight. They are having meetings there now.

There were about 13 at the leap year party and they had a good time they stayed at Gardners. I went to Books Tues eve and played Flinch till about 10 o'clock, then came home. I went to church with Betsy Wed. eve. At Jacksville and after it was over we went to Gardners and played Flinch until about 11:30 and got home in time to escape a thunderstorm.

If I can and it is not raining I think I will call at the Stone House tomorrow eve. and see if Mae is Tempest or Sunshine. Bert was there Friday eve. He rode with me to J.K. Vogans. I was going to Rose Point and then went over from there. He left here about 4 PM and got back a little after 3 AM next day.

It is funny how Frank refers to the book about Tempest and Sunshine that they discussed early on.

Frank is keeping track of every move that Bert makes. I wonder if Bert knows that he is being watched. He continues his report on the hours that Bert is keeping at the Stone House.

He got Dick [the horse] *from Dad this evening and went over again. He allowed they could have church of their own. I could write more but will wait until you tell me whether you wish it or not for I fear you will be disgusted if you had more of the facts.*

Oh my, what is he saying?

If the little bird gets the news given correctly its OK but if not there it had better beware.

Again one is reminded that there is but a step between us and death. 1 Samuel 20:3. by the death of Jim Cleland a young man whom I think you know. He was buried yesterday and his death resulted from picking his teeth, blood poison was result. I think he was at Ira's C."

This scripture says in 1 Samuel 20:3, "But David vowed again, saying, 'Your father knows well that I have found favor in your eyes, and he thinks, 'Do not let Jonathan know this, lest he be grieved.' But truly, as the LORD lives and as your soul lives, there is but a step between me and death."

I have your photo before me and your ring on my finger but that

134

does not satisfy the longings I have for one who is to be away so short (?) a time. May the Father bless and keep you from harm is my prayer. Good night.

He continues the next day with some more small talk.

Mon. 1 PM. It rained about all night. Bert got home about 4 o'clock. He went to the barn and went to sleep in the manger this forenoon. He is cleaning his clothes now. He sends his best in return. How many students do you have now? I am going to go to R.P. [Rose Point] and get my buggy top repaired and will call at the Stone House some time this PM or eve.

I have just finished reading Stepping Heavenward. It is very good. I wish you could of read it before you left. It would of done you good. The church has bought Joe Harlands property for a parsonage.

103.   Martha - Mar. 11, 1904, New Martinsville, W.Va.

We have been having some awful wet weather. I got to see a flood here after all. Last Saturday they rode up and down the streets all day in boats. I got a boat ride too. Rev. Dentin, our minister took three of us girls for a boat ride. It was my first and I enjoyed it so much I think it is grand. Mother thought it was something terrible to see so much water. But every body here seems to have a good time. The water has gone down now. I think there will be no more floods.

Well, this is a case of making lemonade out of lemons. Isn't it something that they would use the flood as a means of pleasure boat riding? "Everybody here seems to have a good time." They certainly looked at things differently a hundred plus years ago.

You ask me how many pupils I had. I have ten. But there will be some that will not commence till after school. There is six that will take now that will be that many to help keep me out of mischief any way for the present.

Was you over to see Mae last Monday? You had better watch out or Bert will get after you. You ask me if I wished to know more of the facts. Was it concerning Mae and Bert if so you bet I want to know them.

Mother is out at my brothers now. She has been gone since last Tuesday morning. She expected to stay a week but I doubt if she gets back in a week.

It was to bad about Jim Cleland, but that is the way with life. We know not when our turn may come to be called to a better home. O yes when you was over to see Mae did you get the lunch at twelve as of old?

CHAPTER 20

STONE HOUSE HAPPENINGS

A lot of paper and ink has been spent on what is going on with Bert and Mae. Mae is Martha's sister and lives at the Stone House. I am not sure if Bert was related to Frank, but we saw that Frank's father lent him a horse to go to the Stone House. He slept in the barn at the Patterson farm and with Frank as well. Martha is very interested in what is going on at the Stone House. Frank continues the episodes in this story line.

104.   Frank - Mar.13, 1904, Slippery Rock, Pa.

Bert is at the Stone House this evening. He was there Thursday night also. I was there last Mon. I went to the front door and rapped 3 times and then went to the kitchen door and as no one heard me I walked in but was met by Mae. I think she was sleeping. But she denied it. Your father had been out and came in soon in a few moments. They are getting along very well but are anxiously awaiting the coming of Mother for what is home without a mother.

I am having many pleasant times. The last was about Feb. 23-4. I am looking forward to more even though they be far apart the greater the cross the brighter the crown.

137

Frank is no doubt referring to the last time he was with Martha before she left for New Martinsville. I take it to mean that the longer he is away from her the greater their reunion will be.

We have a sick sow and when Bert got home last night about 3:30 I got up to see the pig. He was asleep when I got back and as I did not go to sleep for some time I experienced a funny rehearsal. I guess Bert was dreaming for he put his arm around me and there that was proper but after I should have said <u>quit</u> <u>behave yourself</u>. Now be good etc. But I kept quiet so as not to waken him after I got to amused I held his arm he was hugging me with and wakened him. He felt bad of course and said he was after covers. I had intended to call on Mae in the evening but as the roads were bad I changed my mind.

This is so funny and shows that Bert was staying with the Pattersons, even sharing the bed with Frank.

I found out how long Mae must wait for Pappa's consent also something else. Mae and Bert were at Porterville last night. They started the Sun. night before but it got to raining and they came back after going to Tibays. Your father let that secret out.

Portersville is only a couple of miles from the Stone House. I have no idea what the occasion was for them to go there nor do I know what Tibays is and why this should be a secret.

I got a cold reception the kitchen fire had gone out and the setting room fire was about gone.

Are you enjoying yourself as well as you expected and any better than the last time? Are you the organist now and have you got homesick yet? Do you often think of me? Are you getting fat?

What a funny question to ask. But the important one, the one he really wants an answer to, is whether she thinks about him often.

I think of you very often and last night I drempt [sic] *you and I were at some gathering and some one was trying to get you & some others drunk. I found it out and gave you a signal that saved you.*

I love this, that Frank dreamed that he saved Martha, a member of the Temperance movement, from getting drunk. What a dream!

105.   Frank - Mar 15, 1904, Slippery Rock, Pa.

This is not a letter as the others have been but a short essay sent to Martha so I include it here. I am always amazed by my grandfather's use of language. I hadn't heard punctuation used this way before so I looked it up and sure enough, it can mean something that contrasts or accentuates. Martha never refers to this essay in her subsequent letters.

"For Punctuation of a Good man to a Bad man"

He is an old man and experienced in vice and wickedness, he is never found in opposing the works of iniquity, he takes delight in the downfall of his neighbors, he never rejoices in the prosperity of his fellow creatures, he is always ready to assist in destroying the peace of society, he takes no pleasure in serving the Lord, he is uncommonly diligent in sowing discord among his friends and acquaintances, he takes no pride in laboring to promote the cause of Christianity. He has not been negligent in endeavoring to stigmatize all public teachers, he makes no effort to subdue his evil passions, he strives hard to build up Satan's kingdom, he lends no aid to the support of the gospel among the heathens, he contributes largely to the devil, he will never go to heaven, he must go where he will receive his just recompense and reward.

106.   Martha - Mar 16, 1904, New Martinsville, W.Va.

Martha does not respond to Frank's essay in this letter or any of the following letters. She answers some of his many questions. He wants to stay connected by knowing what she is doing.

I have three lessons to give this afternoon, so I will be busy three hours any way.

I was at prayer meeting last night and we have choir practice after that. I am not regular organist as I don't wish to be. I played last Sunday morning and also last night for prayer meeting. I sing in the choir, you can imagine you hear my melodious voice. How are you getting along with your voice? Can you sing as good as ever and who is your teacher now? I should not ask that question. You can omit it if you wish.

You surely don't think I am homesick yet and have only been here three weeks today. I haven't had time to get homesick yet. You spoke of the roads being bad. You have one thing to be thankful for. And that is that you don't have to make any trips at the Stone House after night and probably up set in the mud.

Martha does not respond like Frank would like her to. He wants to hear that she is homesick. She is a little sarcastic because she knows that Frank would especially love being able to take the muddy roads over to the Stone House any time, even at night.

Mae said she was very much surprised to see you coming over. You might of told me that something else you heard of Mae and Bert. I guess it is pretty near time mother is going home. They have things to much their own way. I would just like to be at home now, if I wouldn't have some fun. We are expecting mother in the this week. Charles is coming in with her.

Martha thinks the two love birds are alone too much at the Stone House, and they need mother there to chaperone.

107.   Martha - Mar 17, 1904, New Martinsville, W.Va.

Two days later she writes again to acknowledge the books Frank sent to her.

I have just rec'd to books, and I know that you are the means of there coming. And there is a little difficulty in the one Stepping Heavenward. They do not have it in stock and they wanted me to send for another one it's value instead. So I am going to send you this slip or letter they wrote me, for I do not just understand it. I presume you are the one that has been sending for them so I will send it to you. I received "Lena Rivers" and "Wife in Name Only" and of course it is all unawares to me and I don't know what it means and I presume you will know. If you sent them, I thank you many times. I will have something to keep me busy for a while. I was just down at the post office and put a letter in for you, and rec'd the books. So I suppose you will get too letters this week. I think you ought to be satisfied.

As noted before, when Frank and Martha spoke about the book, "Tempest and Sunshine," it is nice to see what they were reading . "Lena Rivers" is by the same author, Mary Jane Holmes and "Wife in Name Only" is by Charolette M. Brame. I was able to get all the books that are mentioned. It is fun to read these books and notice the proper language and etiquette they used over a century ago.

CHAPTER 21

SO MANY FRIENDS

Frank is a young man and he is not staying home with his parents all the time. He enjoys going out to parties and playing games with his friends. Although Martha is always on his mind, he keeps busy with his friends. He is not out drinking and dancing or gambling, but just having nice clean fun.

108.   Frank - Mar.18, 1904, Slippery Rock, Pa.

Margaret and I have been at Margaret Book's this evening playing Flinch. Ben Harlan had come after Josephine and Oran and Pearl Brandon were there we played 8 hand game but it is to many to be enjoyed very much. They sang some but I did indulge.

I have just as good a voice as ever but I am like a sheep with out a shepherd. I have no one to teach me what to do.

Margaret Book is going to have a picnic next Tues. Nora will have an entertainment at her school next Fri. night. She will teach a select school at Harlensburg after she finishes hers. There is also a lecture at Plaingrove next Fri. night. If it is a nice evening I may go to one of the places, probably Plaingrove. I was at Rose Point again this am with Dick. I have not been in the bank since you were in with me.

He gets back to the subject of what Martha is doing for a short paragraph and then back to the gossip in Butler County, Pennsylvania.

Where does Charley live that she returned to N.M.? [New Martinsville] *I thought she would be on her road home when there? You forgot some of my questions last letter.*

Joe Davis is going with Emma pretty strong. Billy was here last Wed. night. Margaret thinks I am a good bit of a crank. I don't want to go any place any more since you have gone. A grin is beginning to appear on A.M Pounds face. I can't tell how long until he can laugh. I think I told you before that Jim Vogan still goes to Van Horns.

The good friends are divided up into couples, but Frank is the single one, waiting for his love to return.

109.   Martha - Mar 23, 1904, New Martinsville, W.Va.

Mother was getting ready to leave for Pittsburg and I assisted her in every way I could. She left yesterday evening. We haven't heard anything from her yet. I do not know how she got there. She expected to stay there till Thursday and then go to Rochester and stay till Sat. then to New Castle. So you can tell Bert mother is coming home. I have felt lonesome since she left, but I will try and not get homesick so soon at any rate.

Rochester is a small town northwest of Pittsburgh. It was a major junction of the Pennsylvania Railroad and a the home of the National Glass Company. At it's height, it employed a thousand people. The company went bankrupt during the Great Depression.

Martha says that Bert and Mae should get ready to abide by the

143

house rules because Mother is coming home. She admits that she is lonesome now because her mother went home. She doesn't say she is lonesome because she misses Frank, which is what he really wants to hear.

I presume I will half to answer the rest of your questions. I believe you ask me if I thought of you. I would not know why I should not. I often think of where I spent my last afternoon and evening while at home. My mind often runs back to Butler County and especially to <u>one</u>. But I do not want you to stay at home and not enjoy life. Life is to short. I am trying to enjoy myself and I want you to do the same. I believe I answered the rest of the questions in the last letter. If I did not tell me of it. I believe I ask you some that you never answered but I suppose these was not worth while.

She answers the question he wants to hear about, but it sounds cold and again a little sarcastic, "I would not know why I should not" [think about you.] She talks about the places she was before she left, but finally says her mind runs back especially to "<u>one</u>" and she underlines it for emphasis but never really says, I miss you or think about you the way Frank does. Maybe she doesn't want him to stay home pining away for her so she remains stoic in her answer.

Well what are you doing theses days? Are they having any more parties? I suppose that season will soon be over. Did you have a hard storm yesterday evening? It stormed here very hard. It made you think of the good old summer time. I have too lessons to give tomorrow. I have six pupils that are taking right away and the rest will not take till after school. There is two more months of school here yet. It will be out in May. How is Mae and Bert getting along? Does he still go over yet? Does Sam still go with Pearl?

Hoping this finds you well and enjoying yourself. PS. I forgot to tell you I spent last Sunday afternoon or a part of it in Ohio. There was three of us girls went two of my chums and myself. We went across the river in a boat to Baresville. We just went over to see the place and it was such a lovely day. I enjoyed it very much. If there is anything you wish to know and I have forgot to write it tell me of it. Good bye for this time.

CHAPTER 22

BOOKS AND MORE BOOKS

It is very considerate for Frank to send books to Martha. Apparently there was a mail order company where he could order them and have them sent to her. Hmm, sounds like an early Amazon to me.

110.   Frank – March 24, 04, Slippery Rock, Pa.

I have been looking for a better yesterday and today and as I have been thinking a great deal about you, I am going to start a letter. I sent a letter to town with Father last Sat as I will this one, and on Sat. evening I received the note and an order for a book. I happened to have a list such as was required and I sent for a book which I hope will be as good as the one you did not get. Mother said she will give you hers to read. In place of 'Stepping Heavenward,' you will receive either 'Imitation of Christ' or 'Mine own People.' I did not know which would be the best. I hope you will enjoy the other books. I enjoy Lena Rivers the other I have never read. I suppose you wonder how I am enjoying 'Reveries of a Bachelor.' Bert said Mae was going to tell you I was reading it. I took the book out of the shelf and read the preface then put the book up and have not looked at it since.

Out if extreme curiosity I purchased the book "Reveries Of A Bachelor, Or A Book Of The Heart" by Donald Grant Mitchell. The first copyright is 1850 but now available through Forgotten Books. As I leafed through the book I did not see anything very offensive by today's standard but more amusing. It seems that this young man is daydreaming about what marriage would be like. I will quote a paragraph where he is thinking about her looks. "Perhaps she is ugly; not noticeable at first, but growing on her, and (what is worse) growing faster on you. You wonder why you didn't see that vulgar nose long ago; and that lip–it is very strange, you think, that you ever thought it pretty. And then, to come to breakfast, with hair looking as it does, and you not so much as daring to say, "Peggy, do brush your hair!" Her foot too-not very bad when decently chaussée-but now since she's married she does wear such infernal slippers! And yet for all this, to be prigging up for an hour when any of my old chums come to dine with me!"

Frank drastically changes the subject. I am curious as to why he is interested in the Presbyterian denomination.

Caroll W. and I sent for some Presbyterian literature and I am now reading that they have some very good arguments, but I am solid for some time yet.

Bert was over to see Mae last Sun. eve., he was also there last night. And I suppose will be again on Sun. night. They were at Rose Point to church there this week. He says he and Mae walked down the aisle holding the singing book and stood around the alter. He enjoys himself so much with Mae. He told me the other day that it was pretty serious at the S.House. He has put off gig to the lakes for a while. I would love to be at the Stone House for a while with my friend in New M. [New Martinsville] but I suppose I must not complain so I will say nothing more about it now.

I was in the coal bank and dug some coal last Mon. The first time I was in since you were in. Everything is in good shape except the track. I run the car full of coal off twice and I will fix it before I dig any more which may be some time in the future. I have been working in the orchard for a few days since. We have made over two gallon of maple molasses and you can just bet I am getting sweet.

I don't think it will be long until A M Pounds will wear a smile. There is no Grantboro news worth sending except Dame rumor reports a wedding soon. I think it must be Bert and Mae. Good night, Your Hubby I wish I had you to make me a lunch.

Such a sweet way he signs his letter. He adds to his letter the next day.

Roy and Caroll stopped from the picnic and played Flinch. That something else I found out was told you a few lines below where it was mentioned. However it was of no importance. I have an invitation to call on a music teacher some evening. My voice needs training so I guess I will go, if it don't rain, as you will be entirely out the picture with me if I don't practice some. I only wish you could hear me sing now.

Bert wants to now[sic] if you have seen any snakes yet. He said he meant rattle snakes. Remember the Zoo in Highland Park.

I used to go to this zoo as a child and of course took my children and grandchild there, never giving a thought that my grandparents also went there as young people. "The Pittsburgh Zoo opened on June 14, 1898, a Highland Park Zoo, after Christopher Lyman Magee donated $125,000 (about four million dollars when adjusted for inflation) for the construction of a zoological garden in Pittsburgh's Highland Park. Like most other zoos of the time, the Pittsburgh Zoo more closely resembled a menagerie than an actual zoo. However, as time progressed, the animal exhibits eventually became more naturalistic, and the zoo's goal became more focused on conservation."[21]

Sam is still going with Pearl. Jim with May. Margaret said Hello and hung up the receiver. Morning test I suppose. Bert and I killed 2 calves today, got one of John Payne the others at Bill Davis. I am trimming apple trees now. I take a look at the Stone House every once in a while but the charm is gone. I hope you are enjoying City Life. I am contented where I am and expect to be more so in the "Good Old Summertime." That is if my hopes materialize. There has not been any parties since the one the 22? I don't know of any coming either.

111.   Martha - Mar 30, 1904, New Martinsville, W.Va.

I do not include the opening paragraph because they are usually the same, but this letter shows that Martha really wanted to be with him. Frank always wanted her to admit that she had the "blues" or was homesick for him.

I again will take the pleasure to answer your welcome letter which was rec'd. I was as usual glad to hear from you. I guess I have the blues and feel lonesome today and thought I would devote part of the day in talking to you if it is only on paper. I know that will suit you just as well when it cannot be other wise.

I am awful glad that you have taken such an interest in your voice. I hope it will be greatly improved when ere we meet, if that chances to be. I had a letter from Mae the same time I received yours. She said she wished Mother would hurry up home. I guess she has had a great deal of company besides Bert.

Mae told me about you reading the "Reveries of a Bachelor." She thought it looked pretty bad. I am glad you changed your mind and put it back upon the shelf. I have been reading the books you sent me. They are very interesting. I have read "Wife in Name Only"

---

[21]From Wikipedia "Pittsburgh Zoo & PPG Aquarium"

through. There is some parts of it very sad. I enjoy "Lena Rivers" the best. I have not read it through yet but I enjoy reading it. I thank you very much for your kindness in sending them.

Are you going to turn to a Presbyterian? You would make a much better <u>Methodist.</u> You can tell Bert I have seen some very charming snakes and he must not make of W.Va. like that. I have not heard from Mother since she was Pittsburg. [sic] I have just been wondering if she got home all right.

I will proceed to answer a few of the questions you ask me. I have got rid of my cold and am not a bit sorry for it seems I have had a cold all winter. I do not know whether I weigh any more or not. I have never been weighed since I came out here but I do not eat any more than when at home so I do not think I weigh any more. Do you still have your good appetite? I am enjoying city life very well. Sorry you can not enjoy it with me. There is still a few pimples will come out on my face. It would be something new if there wasn't. I believe that is all the questions. If you have more ask them the next time. Do you play flinch very much any more? I have played a few games since here. Last Mon. Mr. Blacks bookkeeper stopped here for dinner and to wait for the five o'clock train out to his work. He had been home. So we played three games. I only got the game once. You know what a good player I am.

CHAPTER 23

NOT SO APRIL FOOLED

Frank got a big kick out of trying to play an April Fool's joke on Martha. He did the same thing to the postman by writing the state first, then the town and finally her name. We will see that his efforts were not appreciated by Martha.

112.   Frank – April 1, 04, Slippery Rock, Pa.

This letter is written sideways on the paper and he is literally writing between the lines. It was very hard to transcribe. He did this for an April fool's joke. I have to give him credit for being original in this idea and I think it took quite and effort on his part. Hmm, let's try it!

I was not April fooled once today. Your letter came to hand yesterday and I was pleased
Do you have any special way of putting your letter in the envelopes? Can you read
to hear from you and to know that you got your letter off a day sooner, may it be likewise
between the lines. Bert has Mae's picture in the frame along side of yours, his is right
this time. When do you get this epistle? Do you get mail on the

151

Sabbath? How may

above it. What does Laura think of you still keeping that old hayseed for a beau or does

pianos have you sold? How many pupils have you now?Do you take an interest in church

she know it? Do you wear the gold band? I have yours on my finger each night. Would

work? Do you ever hear from Sandy Hook? Maybe that ain't the right name. I forgot.

you not like to be home?

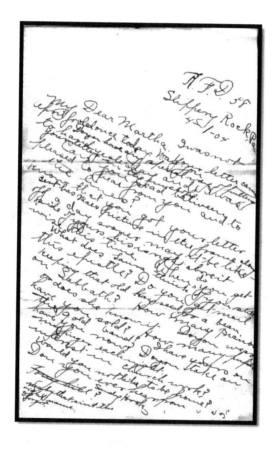

He stopped writing between the lines, but is still writing sideways on the paper.

Don't forget to answer any of these questions as they are all important. Don't fail to write more than the answers. This has been a very wet day, it begun to rain last night about 10:30 and the runs are very high.

Pennsylvania dialect uses words, like "the run," that are not common elsewhere so here is a note of explanation, and by the way, the word "runs" is not in the dictionary. A run is a very small stream usually about three feet wide. There were several running through the fields at the farm that I could jump over as a child. I looked this up in Wikipedia. The only thing I found was, "The Run is a <u>stream</u> in the <u>Dutch</u> <u>province</u> of Noord-Brabant." I wonder if that is the origin of this word?

He is now writing normal.

The day I was at Plaingrove with Sam, I decided to get some Pres. [Presbyterian] literature. I have not found any truths yet capable of convincing me that I should follow that church. If I could find proof that the Methodists were nearest right in their belief I can go to them willingly.

Bert was over at your old home last night and last Sun. night. Mother don't help things very much. He got home about six o'clock this morning. I think from what I can learn our past has been pretty well rehearsed, that is our sayings.

Father bought a pair of good table cloths from an Irish peddler that stops here once in a while for the one that gets married first. (M. B, or me). Who do think will get it? Margaret had a letter from Sadie Weiners and she will not be married until August.

We play Flinch once in a while now but not as often as we used to. I expect to eat about 1 doz. eggs for Easter.

I can't write like I used to and if you think things are a little mixed

153

up just consider that I am an Oddfellow. I have not been at Portersville since before you left. I am real sick and want you to come home. Your Hayseed Hubby Frank

He ends his letter on a very sweet note, but that does not seem to matter to Martha.

113.   Martha - April 7, 1904, New Martinsville, W.Va.

Oh my, Frank's April Fool letter really backfired. She is madder than a hornet and tells him about it.

I suppose you was disappointed today when the mailman came. But it is all you own fault. I have been all this time trying to read your letter. I was real mad, it was well you was not <u>handy</u>. I had a whim not to write at all this week. I am hardly over it yet, but I repented for you said you was real sick. I think you must be bedfast or else wrote that when you was <u>asleep</u>. Pardon me for speaking thus. You know what I mean.

Well to change the subject, I had a letter from Mae, just got through reading it. She said Chester was going to have a social. I suppose you will attend. I am sorry I can not accompany you, but no doubt you are just as well satisfied. That is the first letter I have received from home since Mother went home. I had begun to think they had forgot me, but I guess they had not. I guess Mae has some one else to think about instead of me.

Of course, she is talking about Bert.

We have lots of work to do now. We have begun to clean house. The paper men has been here today and papered three rooms and there is four more to paper so I suppose they will be here all week.

I remember that so many of the old houses from the beginning of the century had wallpaper. They were usually flowers and stripes.

154

I am going to iron in the morning and I give a lesson tomorrow. I am getting along very well with my scholars. I helped to sell one piano or I just went with the parties who got it to help them to pick one. The music man, Mr. Bee gave me three or four pieces of music. There is a music recital at the church tonight but I did not care to go.

Easter is past for another year. We had very good meeting here during the day. The Sunday School alone raised thirty-nine dollars and sixty-five cents for missions and with the church collection making over fifty dollars. I think that was real good.

One dollar in 1904 is equal to 28.85 in 2019. In other words, $1 in 1904 is equivalent in purchasing power to about $28.85 in 2019, a difference of $27.85 over 115 years.[22] That would be a good offering today.

I think I will have to contradict myself in the first part of the epistle for if you intended to eat one dozen of eggs, you can not be feeling very bad. Ha ha

I will not attempt to answer the questions in this letter. I will wait till you ask me the rest then I will answer them all at once. I feel very sorry that Polly was sick. But I hardly think I was the cause of it so that will not worry me any. I am enjoying myself here very much and enjoy being here. I do not know as yet when I shall be home, but I know some sweet day I will be in the family circle again on the Stone House on the hill. There is a great deal of sickness here in town and a great many deaths so many children dying of measles and pneumonia. There was a man hung himself in the jail Sat. They was going to take him to the poor farm and put him in there till it was convenient to take him but he ended it all.

Hoping I haven't written anything to make you feel bad. If I have

---

[22]CPI Inflation Calculator

you can consider I am the same cranky Martha

114.   Frank – April 11, 04, Slippery Rock, Pa.

I will try and write a few lines this evening which I trust may be more legible than my last one. In beginning I wish to say that I got exceedingly tired waiting on your reply and I hope it may not be so again for a while. I have always been prompt and expect you to be like wise but since you were cleaning house I will remember my sorrow no more. Don't say that I am a crank.

He really doesn't get it. The letter was late in coming, and it was his own fault! He only refers to this letter being more legible but doesn't acknowledge how angry she was, and he has the nerve to scold her for being long in answering.

I have been helping to get a potato patch ready to plow these last few days. Last Thurs. I was dynamiting stumps. There was plenty of noise and lots of pleasure seeing stumps fly into the air.

Margaret and I went to Chesters entertainment. He had his graphaphone there after he played his pieces the girls went behind the curtains and stuck their hand through the curtain and the boys bid there for partners. I eat with Pearl Vanhorne (45cents). Sam brought her and Jim brought May V.

Your sister Mae was there but Bert was not. I suppose he did not want to spend his money. However he did get extravagant sometime since and got Mae a box of chocolates. He is working for Mack and Port Books now. He appears well contented. He's among good Presbyterians now.

Don't put yourself to any trouble to answer my questions. I am thinking of calling at the S.H. Some time soon and perhaps your mother can tell me some of the things I wished to know. I have longing for to see the old home again and to see if I am as welcome as I used to be.

Grandmother has not been well for some time so I have not been at church at Harlensburg for some time. They will have church all the time after June first.

Tues. I started to plow this morning but stopped about 10 am on account of severe snow storm.

I don't think of any thing to interest you like your letters do me and if there is any thing you would like to know of let me know and I will reply at the earliest possible opportunity. I am still ignorant as to where that Sweet day will be when you are home. The Almanac don't give it.

CHAPTER 24

BUSY SCHEDULES

115.   Martha - April 15, 1904, New Martinsville, W.Va.

After a long sentence about receiving his letter, she concludes a paragraph with the following.

You have more to write than I have and I enjoy reading your letters. I know they are more interesting than mine is.

I am selling tickets for an entertainment next Thurs eve. There is a man coming here, he is a great pianist. He is coming for the benefit of the League. So we was each one assigned twenty five tickets to sell. I have sold four. I will sell what I can and the rest I will take back. They are a quarter a ticket.

I hope you enjoy yourself when you go over home. Tell them that you heard from me and I am just the same. I received a letter from Mother this week. I was somewhat surprised to get a letter from her but I highly appreciated it. She told me all about her visit. She enjoyed herself very much. You can ask her all the questions you like no doubt she would answer them better than I would.

Well Frank I do not like to cease writing yet, but I will half to go and get ready for school will soon be out and I presume if you still think I am as slow as I use to be. I had better quit writing and go get ready.

Martha signs her letters, "Sincerely yours." Not the sweet "Your Hubby or Hubbie" that Frank signs.

116.   Frank – April 18, 1904, Slippery Rock, Pa.

I started to plow in the field below the hill this morning and broke my plow then went to Harlansburg and got repairs and a new plow too, so we have two plows now.

Things haven't changed much in over a hundred years. You go to the store for one thing and end up with two. This made me laugh.

Marg and I are going to Dambaughs tomorrow evening. Nora is 21 and as we owe them a visit we will return it then. Wed eve the auditors meet at J. K. Vogans.

Thurs eve I am expected to be at prayer meeting at Nick Gardners. Fri. evening vacant yet. Sat Eve. Marg and I at Rollins. This will perhaps be part of my diary for this week.

Frank writes about his activities in a very matter of fact way, almost like he is showing Martha that he is doing fine without her. His life goes on in a very busy fashion. He is not pining away missing her.

He continues the story she is most interested in, Bert and Mae. This is all strange to me because this was in the day that staying overnight together without marriage was not a common thing. This reminded me of the time my husband and I were staying in Amish country near Lancaster, Pa. We were awoken several nights by the sound of horse clip clop and carriage wheels turning. We inquired as to why anyone would be out at 2 am. We were told that it was

Amish boys going home from seeing their girlfriends. We were very surprised that the Amish were just like other people, staying out late. Of course, I think in either case there was nothing but innocent time together.

I saw Bert today. He said he just got home this morning when they were calling him to get up. He did not get to bed on Thus night either. I see where I could improve.

I enjoyed myself quite well at the Stone House Sat. eve. I went to the kitchen door and remained in the setting room. I missed the midnight lunch. They would not believe me when I told them I had not heard from you for a week. I guess they thought you should do better. I did not learn all I would like to know so I suppose I will have to go in ignorance.

CHAPTER 25

ATTITUDE

Frank's trick from the April Fools letter caused dissension between them. She did not appreciate his shenanigans in making her read "between the lines," and it caused her several days to interpret it.

She may be feeling insecure because he is so busy with all his friends, and forgotten their good times when they were together.

117.   Martha - April 22, 1904, New Martinsville, W.Va.

I have just came home from church and thought I would try and answer your letter before retiring. This has been a lovely day and a beautiful evening. It makes one think of the good old summertime.

Martha starts a long paragraph about the timing of the letters. Frank mentioned that she took too long in replying to his letter. He was busy but took time to answer promptly. It sounds like she took offense when she comes back with the following.

When you have more important business to tend too as you spoke of in your letter. I do not wish to detain you that way you write to me when you have nothing else to do.

This attitude continues as she writes about his visit to the Stone House.

I am very glad you enjoyed yourself over home. No doubt you enjoyed yourself better than if I had of been there. I am sorry you did not get the lunch but I presume you did not ask for it as you use to of old. I had a letter from Mae. She told me all about your visit. They was very glad to see you.

I think you might of told me of the lots I had to write about. I suppose you think I don't answer your questions any way but I am going to fool you tonight. I am going to answer all you have ever ask me in your letters.

She starts on the answers very matter-of-factly.

I have helped to sell one piano, I have nine scholars now. I hope to get more after school is out. There is just three more weeks. And I take as much interest in church work as I ever did, if you would of saw me last wk. You would of thought so.

We had entertainment in the school house last night. Mr. Guss he is a graduate of Europe in music. He came and give a recital for the benefit of the League. He was assisted by three others. I thought it was very good. The League made about twenty-five dollars clear money.

Lena Bandi and I, that is a girlfriend of mine, were appointed of the League to go around and get advertisements of businesses for on the programme. We charged fifty and seventy five cents a space. We made twenty dollars in that way.

The attitude continues. I think she is more homesick and lonely for him than she wants to admit.

Well I must proceed with the questions or I won't get them answered. Yes I wear that with my initials on. When ever you wish me not to, tell me.

And Laura also knows I have the Butler Co. farmer yet too. I do not know what you meant about Sandy Hook. I never hear from anyone but you. But I am going to hear from someone else soon. I guess you can get mail here on Sabbath but I always think I can wait till Monday. And I never go to the office on Sun.

I believe that is the amount of the questions now. You ask all you wish to and I will try and answer them more prompt. And don't forget the news you have for me in next letter. You might of told me in this letter but I think you just told me that so I would write sooner. I am sorry you will not receive this epistle sooner but indeed I could not help it. Will try and do better after this.

It is hard to imagine that they would be so busy that it is hard to find time to write a letter. No cell phone, internet, or television. But on the other hand, no dishwasher, washer and dryer, and no automobile. Hmm, maybe it evens out.

I have three lessons to give tomorrow. I give one this evening. I give them mostly after school now.

I am having a fine time down here. Last Sunday was such a beautiful day. There was several of us went out for a walk. We are planning to enjoy the river some this summer I think. It is fine amusement to boat ride.

118.   Frank – Apr. 26, 04, Slippery Rock, Pa.

Yours of the 22ⁿᵈ received yesterday evening. Your last letter was answered the same evening it was received and I think if you refer to it again you will see that it was the date you wrote on that was referred to.

163

I included this opening paragraph to show that the timing of the letters is an ongoing discussion.

I went to Uncle Smiths at N. Liberty Sun. evening and did not get back until late last evening. I would have answered then but did not get a chance. My cousin Dewit P. is here this evening so I do not have as much time as I would like. I am glad to see you have reformed in regard to answering questions.

Is Frank showing a little attitude too? I notice that there has not been very much talk about their faith. They talk of church activities but not like the sweet time when they were reading the same scriptures at the same time or the reminder to one another that they are praying for each other. It seems that busy schedules without including the Lord can lead to poor attitudes.

There was a heavy rainstorm here Sun. eve so there was no church. I was greasing my harness today. There will not be much more plowing this week on account of the wet weather that is present.

My last weeks diary was filled up to perfection. This one will be as full.

Now he sweet talks her to make her feel better.

I want to call to your remembrance some of the pleasures of the past. Some of our drives when we went to sleep, upset, and unhitched together with which the little gray mare played a prominent part. No more will I drive her to the Stone House. No more can you expect to clean white hairs off of your clothes on account of her and no more will I proudly call her my own. She has gone but is not forgotten.

Sooner or later we must all part and may it always be said of thee

Well done, thou good and faithful servant.

Owing to the fact that we need two barns, I was obliged to go and seek a new horse as many seek new girls. At last I got a fine colt 3 years a bay. He is about a foot taller than Polly and will make an extra nice looking driving horse when he gets slicked up and broke. He has never been hitched single yet. He weighs 1005# now. His name is "Prince." I am anxious to know who will have the first pleasure trip behind him.

Walker Book came and bought Polly last Fri. at noon. I expect to miss her a good bit for a while but as I have not much running at night to do I guess I can get along.

Mother and Margaret are papering the setting room today. It has been raining very near all day and I am going to grease another set of work harnesses.

I can't think of as much to write as I would like but hope to do better next time. I am pleased to know you still wear my gift. I wear yours each night and when I go away. We are all well and hope you are also. Have you received that last book if not please let me know.
Your Hubby
Frank
PS When you go boat riding please don't go near the water or you may get baptized before you are ready. FVP

I wanted to include his post script, because it is humorous. Frank is a Baptist and they believe in full immersion as an adult or at least able to decide for oneself to be baptized. Martha is a Methodist and they sprinkle the head of the baby with the decision for baptism being the parent's responsibility. However, Martha eventually does get baptized by immersion because she was a member of Zion Baptist Church and that was membership requirement.

119.   Martha – May 1, 1904, New Martinsville, W.Va.

I have just came home from church and thought I must answer your most welcome letter before retiring for the night. I was out walking all afternoon with some other girl friend. It was such a beautiful day for walking. We must of walked a mile or two for I know I am awful tired. I presume you think if I was home I would not want to walk to Rose Point. But I have traveled that road so often. I went over some ground today that I never seen before so it was interesting and I enjoyed the walk.

I suppose that was the news you had to tell me was selling Polly, that noble horse. I do not see how you could part with her but I presume it will be like friends parting there are some forgotten after a time. I often think how we might have been killed had she been a fraction horse but I shall always remember her for the noble part she played.

She might of meant a race horse. "Fractions are the times for each segment of a thoroughbred horserace. For example, if a horse runs the first quarter mile in 26 seconds and the half mile in 54 seconds, those are considered to be relatively slow fractions."[23]

Is Bert still working at Books yet? I am invited out to play Flinch Tues evening of this week. I haven't played very much since I came down here. I could beat you though. I mean once in a great while. I don't suppose the crocinole (I do not know whether that is spelled right or not) [Crokinole] *board will get very much of a rest.*

---

[23] Answers .com

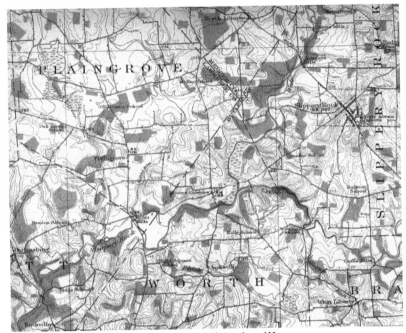

Slippery Rock and Jacksville area
U.S. Geological Survey Map 1913

CHAPTER 26

CHANGE IN DEMEANOR

Finally, they are not chastising one another for the letters being late. They are back to the normal reporting about what they are doing, so Frank thinks.

120.   Frank - May 4, 1904, Slippery Rock, Pa.

I wish to say in the beginning that your letter was the most appreciated of your several letters I think you must of prioritized it.

I have been plowing and harrowing with Prince today. I think he will make a much more desired horse than Polly. You may almost think I didn't think much of the grey mare but I did hate to see her go down the road, never more to be mine but as you say, it's like friends parting.

I remember one friend I parted with and I now ceased to think of her. I found another, and that one is <u>much</u> *better and I hope will continue.*

Does this mean that Frank had a girlfriend before Martha? It sure sounds like he did. But Martha is the one he plans to be with forever.

So far I have remembered your parting directions, Don't use your hands when picking cherries. That was not the words but you can perhaps remember the original.

Whatever is he talking about? We will never know.

Bert is still at Books and he and Mae were at Zion Sun. eve. As he was starting home I wondered if he was going back to the waters so I stopped and said, when are you going back? Several heard me and I guess they all thought I meant to the S.H. For Mae and Bert both blushed and I got no satisfactory answer.

Sun. morning the preacher was making some remarks from Phil 3:19 [Their end is destruction, their god is their belly, and they glory in their shame, with minds set on earthly things.] *and he used plain language and spoke of some peoples belly's being their god that is they want short sermons so as to get home to dinner early. After church Grace G. was complaining about being hungry. I reminded her of what the Rev. R. said and told her she must not let her belly be her god. I was greatly amused to see her blush, not expecting her to.*

So if I am to get any one to help me break Prince, I must not say much or I ll make them blush. I imagine I hear you say you had better be careful what you are talking about.

Now here comes the letter that Frank does not want to see. At least Martha is truthful with him and doesn't get his hopes up for a quick return.

121. Martha - May 10, 1904, New Martinsville, W.Va.

You do not know how busy I am. I am that busy I haven't time to eat and I am getting poor. I am writing to you in the music store this afternoon. I came here last Mon. a week. I like it very much. You would not think I could sell anything, would you? I sell music

169

and all the small goods and also the large goods too. But I haven't as yet had that pleasure of selling a piano although they have sold a great many since I came in and when any one comes in to buy a piano I half to try them over for them. I do not have a great deal to do some days and other days I am pretty busy and then I teach my class in the store.

This is the kind of work I have always wanted. So I am well pleased with it. I come to the store eight in the morning and stay till eight in the evening and an hour at meal time and of course any time I want off they will let me off, that is if I want to go to anything. They are very nice people to work for. There is three men interested in it. The proprietor, salesman and tuner. So that is the news I have for you.

Martha sounds very happy in her work even though the hours are long. She is taking a chance in this honesty with Frank. Career women were few because they were expected to get married and have children. At this time in history women did not have the right to vote.

This letter is not what Frank anticipated, especially when she says, "it is the kind of work I always wanted to do" and "I am is well pleased with it." In his mind, he wants her to give up her career and live in the country as a farmer's wife.

She changes the subject quickly.

We have been having a good bit of sickness at our house the last week. Perry, that is the youngest boy was taken very sick Friday afternoon, but he is better now. Mrs. Black has been very sick all day. I guess she is just wore out waiting the little boy and she has a sore throat. You ought to of seen me hustling around at noon. I had the dinner to get and dishes to wash and I just have an hour. I was at the store when the hour was up. Isn't that a wonder? You always said I was so slow. I have improved somewhat.

Martha is doing her best to help in the current situation of illnesses.

Frank is anxious to write back to her. His heart must have been pounding as he tries to start the letter with the usual small talk but gets to the point rather quickly.

122.   Frank - May 11, 1904, Slippery Rock, Pa.

I am tired but never to tired to read your letters and while it may not be proper yet I am going to answer your epistle this evening which was received but few hours since.

I failed to find your news what you meant for news. Bert was here sometime ago and told me of your exalted position. From the reading of your letter I would judge that you will be more reluctant about coming to the old farm house. I often wonder what you with your wonderful talents can see in me that causes you to even think of me who am nothing but a tiller of the soil. I wish you well but I trust you will not let your work endanger your health.

Frank is having doubts about their future. Why would she want to be with a farmer with her wonderful talents? It is good that she is truthful with him when she tells him how she feels. Frank seems to be belittling himself when he says, "...who am nothing but a tiller of the soil." He is writing with a broken heart. They will have to work this out.

He changes the subject to the usual conversation.

Margaret is back from the City. I guess her visit was enjoyed. Bert left here Sun. for the lakes. He said his "woman" did not want him to go but he told her there was $365 in it and that they would need the money so the money would buy a team of horses and 2 or 3 cows. He does not expect to be back until Dec. that is if he don't go to the bottom.

As mentioned before, Bert is at the lakes. Because he states that he will be gone for several months, it could be Lake Erie, which is approximately ninety mile north. We cannot be certain of this but one thing is sure, he will be making quite a bit of money for their future.

Mae will no doubt think the months are very long and such thoughts as these will often pass though her mind, will he ever get back? Will he remain true? Can I be satisfied to give up my home for such as he can offer? etc. From what Bert says they are quite serious and I heartily wish them many happy years together.

Frank is penning thoughts that could be Mae's, but are they really his thoughts about Martha?

We finished sowing our oats today, corn is the next thing to be rushed after. Frank Book has his planted. Everything in the country is beautiful but soon, oh soon it will pass away to return no more for ever.

News is very scarce and in place of any foolish writing I am going to ask two questions which I trust you will be pleased to answer.

Thurs. The questions I desired to ask, I decided not to send at present and as I have not time for more writing I cut this quick answer short. If you would rather have a long answer long I can make them that way if you desire.

What a letdown. He does not ask the questions? What does he have in mind after writing about Bert and Mae?

123.   Martha - May 16, 1904, New Martinsville, W.Va.

I intended to write yesterday and it was Sunday. But the day was so taken up that I did not get it done. Our church was dedicated yesterday. Dr. Rikes from Mt. Union College preach morning and

172

evening. He is certainly a fine minister. He is going to lecture tonight in the church on the subject, "What shall we do with the boys?" Judging from his sermons yesterday I think it will certainly be good. Last week there was something going on every evening but I guess this week will not be so full.

School was out last week. There was eight graduate of the high school and then the Grammar class graduated to, I do not just know how many was in it. I did not count them. And then we are preparing to hold the district Epworth League convention here the twenty ninth and thirtieth of June. We held a meeting or two last week and then the choir was practicing for the dedication. So the week was all taken up.

Martha gives the usual small talk and then gets down to the main subject. She defends what she has written about her job.

I do not think I think myself any better that other people because I have this position. I am very glad for it and like it very well. But it does not take my thoughts from home. You talk as if you would like to quit writing, or at least that is what I took from it. If you do I would not want you to write to me when you would rather do otherwise. Although I have always enjoyed your letters. But the way you spoke in your letter, I take a great deal of meaning out of it. Mebby I don't do wrong in writing this or even judging your letter that way. Hope you will pardon me if I did wrong.

It sounds like she is saying, this is the way it is, if you don't like it, too bad. She only "enjoyed" his letters. She is a young pretty woman with a very handsome, established, moral, Christian man and she tells him in a sense, it's okay if you don't want to write any more. He didn't say anything in the previous letter about not wanting to write. She is giving him an easy way out if he wants it. They are in a difficult place in their relationship, but God will work it out.

173

No doubt Mae will feel lonesome when Bert left, but that is the way with life. There will be a meeting some day.

Is she trying to encourage him that there will be a meeting with them someday too?

Well Frank it is pretty near train time and I want this to go on this time. Hoping I did not write anything that will make you feel worse.

CHAPTER 27

SERIOUS QUESTIONS

Most of the letters to this point have been cheerful and light-hearted, with family and friends' news and gossip. There have been a few problem issues or disputes, but now there is a turning point in the courtship. Frank has been writing about Bert and Mae, and shows how their relationship is growing stronger. As he reports on "Bert and Mae," he is lonesome for Martha and needs to know if their relationship is also going to move forward.

As seen previously, there has been dialog about country life versus city life. When I opened the following letter, to my surprise, two folded up pictures fell out. One was a picture of a haughty looking city woman and the other was a sweet farmer's wife. He is baring his feelings for Martha.

124.   Frank - May 17, 1904, Slippery Rock, Pa.

Yours dated yesterday received and while I am in doubt as to the propriety in answering so soon yet I trust you will not censure me to hard for it.

I guess I will try and untangle some of my past writings if possible. I guess I had another sick spell and I hope it was not contagious.

As to being tired writing, I think you know that I do not have much love for W.Va. Territory and what I meant was that, I was not tired writing to you but getting tired of you being so far from me. But what right have I to ask you to come handies. I am scarcely more than a friend even though you are the <u>Same</u> as <u>ever.</u> While I expect to be more than a friend in the near future, don't think to hard of the farmer, for this statement.

While I know you do not like to be questioned, I hope you will be lenient with me this time and answer these questions which may appear in this epistle quickly and thoughtfully. You may have noticed that it has been several weeks since I asked a question. Yet I would like to know what your plans for the future are?

There it is, plain and simple. It is what Frank has been wanting to know for a long time. He has to get this off his chest. Are her plans for the future directly related to his future? He continues to explain his feelings.

When you left for the city I understood that you would gone about 3 months, the 3 months will be up next week and you have said nothing about returning. When may I meet you at the station? If for any reason you do not expect to come when you promised, when do you expect to come? I will try and show you that I appreciate your return and I would be most happy to see you. Yet I do not want you to come on my account. Stay until you are perfectly satisfied that you can do no better. Then if it is God's will we shall meet again.

I trust I am not asking to much of you to answer this by return mail. If you cannot answer so I get your reply by Sat. Remember
I will swallow my grief
And await for the leap
That will bring to me joy not sorrow
On one of the few days after tomorrow.

Decoration Day will soon be here and I await your reply so as to know whether your company is to be mine.

He has opened his heart to her and now quickly changes the subject to the usual discourse.

I presume you are making a note of what the wholesale cost is on all musical goods especially pianos. I have not heard a piano playing since you left. I would love to hear the mocking bird. Sweet memories and a few others.

I presume Margaret told you the news. The most important out would no doubt be the arrival of a Miss Stork at the residence of A.M. Pounds. 10#s.

We finished plowing corn ground today with the exception of an acre for fodder corn.

Wed.
I have just been looking at your likeness and I trust there is nothing on these pages that will make the original of that picture frown.

If you can't make out the words between the lines, send it back and I will copy it again.

177

Give my regards to any one inquiring. And remember that even though my writings are not what they should be I mean well and if anything don't suit you don't be afraid to tell me of it. I never cease to pray for you and trust you still remember me.

With love from all to you.
I am faithfully your friend. Frank.

He no longer signs his letters with, "Your Hubby." However he is mentioning the Lord in the letter again, "Then if it is God's will we shall meet again." and reminding her he is praying for her. Yes, it is God who will sort all this out and give Frank the patience he needs.

125.   Martha - May 21,1904, New Martinsville, W.Va.

I am glad you have good health. I suppose you still have your good appetite. I received a letter from Margaret. I was certainly glad to hear from her. Tell her I am going to answer it some of these days. I presume she won't believe it though.

Martha starts out with some small talk, but soon gets to the answers he is not ready to hear.

I will proceed to try and answer your questions but I do not know whether you will get any satisfaction from them or not because my future is blank before me. I have made no plans as yet for my future. I do not make plans and promises and then have them broken. So I am not thinking any thing about it.

As to the promise I made you when I went to New Castle I may of said that but I meant if I did not get in to anything or not succeed in getting up my class. But I have succeeded well since I came here and I have not thought any thing as yet about going home, although many a time I think I would like to run in home and see what they are doing. But I have a good position now. I think I will stay at it for a while. I like it very well and it is something I have always wanted to do and I find much pleasure in it. I came out here for that purpose to do well and to get in to something now that I am getting along alright I do not think it would be right for me to go home when that is what the folks at home sent me out here for.

I could not tell you when to meet me at the station I would like to see you to, but it may be sometime before that pleasure. I am very sorry I made that promise to come home in 3 months. I can not recollect that I said it. I may of said it with reference to what I said before. If it is Gods will we will meet again.

She is answering his questions honestly and bluntly. Her heart is not set on marriage and babies, but on a lovely career in the music field. She is happy, and enjoys success at this stage in her life. She is a strong woman, not intimidated by a promise she does not remember making. She also refers back to God and admits that she is trusting in God to get them together again.

What do you think there was a couple girls came in the store an wanted me to play for a dance tonight, but you know my opinion on that. I told them No and they just coaxed me to just this one night, but I do not care anything for "Satans" pleasures. So I am proud to say No.

I have not thought any think about Decoration Day yet. I forgot all about it till you wrote it. I am sorry to say I can not be in your company. But you can soon find some one else. Margaret said she could not get you to go any place. You must enjoy life while you can. I know I am and you should also. I have been going a good bit I was out to something that would be going on every night this week but last night I stayed at home and finished me a waist.

As I read this, I thought Martha was making a dress. I looked up

179

"waist," I found that according to Webster Dictionary, it referred to "a garment or the part of a garment covering the body from the neck to the <u>waistline</u> or just below." She is possibly making a blouse but we cannot know for sure.

126.   Frank - May 25, 1904, Slippery Rock, Pa.

I am sorry you cannot be home for Decoration. However I hope you will enjoy yourself and as you request I will try and enjoy myself.

I was also much disappointed to know that you had no plans for the future. I trust you may soon have an idea of what you intend to do.

That's it. Plain and simple. No pleading. Now to change the subject and get back to normal composition – work, friends, church, and activities.

We have been very busy with potatoes and corn this week. I was planting corn this evening. Miss Nan Brant Book has another son. There is a report going now that Frank Patterson had a new girl at the memorial services at the Presbyterian church last Sun evening. It may be true and while she was not "Bred in Old Kentucky" yet she lives in Law Co. [Lawrence County] *that she has some attraction for him.*

You may remember that Sam and Jim thinks they have the fastest horses in the county. However they have came to think different now.

Sun. eve was very pleasant for driving and the roads were quite good so I started home on Plaingrove Road. I was ahead with Old Dick and when but a short distance from church they pulled to go around me and remembering that the boys were anxious for little fun I also started a little faster for about two miles. Each tried occasionally to go around me but failed. I hardly think they appreciated it but I couldn't hold Dick.

This is a great narration about Frank's horse, Old Dick, racing the other horses. It reminded me of a story my brother Bill told me that happened in the '60's. He was stopped at a red light in his big body, blue, Pontiac and a guy next to him had a girl with him in a GTO and was revving up his motor. Bill said he could imagine him telling the girl, "Watch me take this big car." When the light turned green, the race was on and of course, my brother won. I hardly think the guy in the GTO appreciated it, but Bill couldn't hold back his big body, blue, Pontiac.

I have got tired being a "Batchelor" and as this is Leap Year I am going to use a portion and see the benefits. I used to think I had plans that would suit you and though I have been disappointed a little yet I am going to wait and in a short time I am going to to ask you a question which will no doubt cause you to make some plans. Now don't get scared it will only be a repetition of one I asked and which you desired to have postponed.

Thurs. This is a wet day so no corn planting today. I gave you an impression of gold dollar which my grandmother gave me this morning. It was one of the first coined, 1849 it is a beauty.

"In 1849, the United States Mint would begin striking the smallest coin it has ever struck to this day – the $1 Liberty Head gold coin. A 13-millimeter, 1.672-gram regular-issue gold coin designed by United States Mint Chief Engraver James B. Longacre (who also designed the Indian Head cent and two-cent coin), this tiny piece was issued in three types over the course of its 1849 through 1889 production period. The gold dollar was instituted just as the Gold Rush kicked off in California and gold became more readily available."[24]

---

[24]COINVALUES.COM

I have got to be a professional man. I take gapes out of chickens. Am quite busy.

This is part of farm life I never knew about. Gapes are, "a disease of birds and especially young birds in which gape worms invade and irritate the trachea."[25]

"A parasitic disease of poultry and other birds, characterized by Frequent gaping due to infestation of the trachea and bronchi with gape worms."[26]

No one has had a ride behind my new horse. I guess I'll take my mother first.

I hope you are well. I look for an early reply. Your last letter was nearer the proper length. Can you still be contented anywhere? Give my regards to any inquiring friends. Write soon. Now for saying to worry your brain. "Don't monkey with the band wagon." I am your friend.

127.　Martha – May 31, 1904, New Martinsville, W.Va.

There are 2 letters with same date in the envelope plus a small newspaper clipping.

I will endeavor to answer your welcome letter which was received

---

[25]Webster Dictionary
[26]Dictionary.com

if you can excuse my lead pencil and I know you will do that for you don't care for my letters anymore by what I hear. But I am going to write anyway. I like to hear from you. I am glad you are having such nice times.

I do not want you to be an old "bachelor" although I still think of our pleasant times together, which I can thank you many many times you showed me, which I was so neglectful to thank you at the time. But I shall remember them. As to be pleased any where, I am willing to go where ever the Lord wants me, although I am not ready yet a while to answer your question. Let us continue to ask God to show us better for another month or two. That is if you care to write to me any more.

Sometimes when there is a difficult decision to make, it is best not to be hasty, but to put it in the hands of the Lord. They having been seeking Him all through this relationship and now, the most important question of all must be according to the Lord's guidance.

I intended to write to you Sunday afternoon but there was several girls came and wanted me to take a walk so I did not get it done and yesterday being Decoration Day I enjoyed the day very much. In the afternoon there was a crowd of us went down to Sisterville, W.Va. in the street car. They have streetcars here to the bridge very near in town so we went down there and stayed till seven o'clock and then in the evening we went to one of my girl friends home to play Flinch. So I didn't get to write yesterday but I hope it will be appreciated any way although I know it can't be as it use to be.

I am kept very busy now days I have hardly time to write to any one but I steal time to write to you and home. There is another girl with me in the store now, so I can have more spare time.

I will try and write more the next time I will try and keep my promise to but I will half to close for this time as it is very near

183

dinner time, and I half to go up home and before I get my dinner I will take a vocal lesson. I commenced last Tuesday. I do not know how I will get a long. How are you getting along with you voice? I suppose you get to take a lesson often now. Well I am sorry but I will half to say Good bye for this time hoping you are well. I await your early reply. Give my best regards to all inquiring friends.
I am As ever the Same,
Martha

I will send you a little slip I found.

CHAPTER 28

ANOTHER GIRL

This is the second letter in the envelope and is very short. It contained a small newspaper clipping which said, "Frank Patterson and Miss Belle Dean attended the Memorial services at Harlansburg, Sabbath evening."

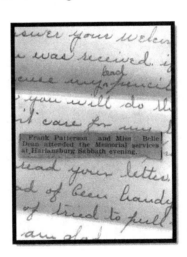

I will endeavor to answer your welcome letter which was received. If you can excuse my lead pencil and I know you will do that for you don't care for my letters now. I was a little provoked when I

read you letter. I believe if I had of been handy I would of tried to pull your hair. I am glad you are having pleasant times but there is one thing, I do not want you to ask that question you spoke off in your letter yet. I do not wish to answer it yet. Wait a month.

Martha was really upset with Frank. The green monster of jealousy is poking out of sweet Martha. She doesn't want to go home but she doesn't want anyone else to have him either.

128.   Frank- June 1, 1904, Slippery Rock, Pa.

Your letter would convey the idea that you are having pleasure in thinking that your letters are not as much enjoyed as they used to be. However I trust you were bluffing for I appreciate them very much and eagerly await their arrival.

Yes. I took Belle to S.R. [Slippery Rock] to the play while it did not rain all the time as it used to do when <u>you</u> and <u>I</u> went driving. Yet the roads were equally as muddy. I did not think the play was as good as some I have been at.

Belle is a fine girl. I enjoy her friendship and trust she enjoys mine. However you or anyone else need not have any fears of her becoming my wife. For we are not suited to each other. There is a saying that there is as good fish in the sea as has been caught and while it may be so yet a person could fare a great deal worse than to take Belle Dean.

It will soon be three years since we met. And as I have met several girls, I have found none whom I thought was suited to me for a helpmeet better than you.

Three years is a good while to fish for consort – if I may use that term, and I now feel that the time has come for me to <u>land</u> the <u>fish</u> or <u>brake</u> the <u>line</u>.

186

I may be hasty, but you know me. I need no introduction in repeating the question which I asked last fall, which answer you would call binding. I again ask if you will be my wife? This answer will be final. And as you request I am willing to give you this month in which to answer. Therefore please remember that if I receive no answer to that question by June 30, 04, I will know that I have lost my <u>sweetheart</u> and July 4th will commemorate no meeting and Aug. 25,04 will be no desired wedding day.

You may think I am rather hasty. Just trying to bring you home when you have got a good position and every thing going, nice but if I were to wait three of four months more your environments would still be greater.

I remember once you told me that a month or two were enough to be engaged. I must say no more on the subject until I get an answer.

Plain and simple, Frank has his ideas on the subject of marriage and nothing is going to change his mind. He is anxious for a positive response.

I was at Rose Point this morning with some cattle we sold and I met Bert E. driving your Father's grey mare. I think he must be staying there. I think he must not have gone to the lakes. I did not have time to talk to him.

Margaret told me to tell you that she did not believe you would keep your word in answering her letter. Margaret and I are invited to a surprise party of Vogans for Jim on the 10th. He will be 20 years.

I am not having my voice trained any. I have no instructor but I expect one by July 4. I trust you will try and be able to begin teaching me by that time if not before. If you have no intention of coming home then I trust you will let me know a day or two before.

187

Thurs.
I had a dream about you last night. We were together once more.
The dream did not last very long.

I trust these few lines finds you well. I have answered as prompt as
I could and hope you may do the same.

Remember I leave this question with you and may God direct you
in answering. I am not perfect by any means yet I hope you may be
able to give an answer which in after years you may never regret.
I am Your Hubby,
      Frank

Frank too recognizes the importance of trusting God in this matter
but seems to use more gentile persuasion. And he is still so hopeful
in signing, Your Hubby.

CHAPTER 29

HARD ANSWERS

The ball is again in Martha's court. She must answer in a way that Frank will understand and decide she is worth waiting for. What difference can a few months make?

129.   Martha - June 6, 1904, New Martinsville, W.Va.

I will try and answer your welcome letter this evening. I did not have to stay in the store tonight. The other girl takes a turn about staying in the evening. I had thought of sewing this eve. but took another notion and thought I would spend the evening in writing to you. But I will not pretend to answer your question this time which I really think you was hasty in asking still I presume I can not blame you. Still I am not ready to answer and it has made me feel bad to think you give me so short a time. I wish you was here this evening to talk to you instead of writing. There is lots of things I would like to tell you which I do not like to write. Although I can not wait your coming as of old I am going to write just a few things I have to say and then you can destroy the letter or keep it where no one will get it. I would much rather you would destroy it.

I had a hard time including this because she specifically asks him to destroy the letter. It shows that it was very hard for her to write because she must follow her heart and do what she thinks is best for her, after all, she is only twenty-two years old. But as we see, Frank did not destroy the letter and it is here as part of their story.

Frank I think of you often and never cease to think of the many pleasant time we spent together and the many glad times you always tried to show me which I appreciated very much and often think I would love to see you. But I do not want to get married yet, I have a good position I get $5.00 a week in the store then I have about ten scholars. I feel I do not want to give then up now. I have just got them rightly started. And you seem to be in a great hurry. You even set the date. So I suppose you will not wait any longer and it will mean quit, though I know it will be a sad parting. We had went together for so long.

Do not think I found pleasure in thinking you did not appreciate my letters for I did not. I really did think it and I was not bluffing as you give me this month to answer. I will not say any more on the subject tonight.

Tues. I did not get this finished last night as I hoped to. I wanted to get this off this morning but failed to do so and I gave two lessons this morning and other work to do. I did not get it off. But trust you will not be disappointed. I tried to answer as soon as I could Probably you will notice different kind of ink. I am writing with the ink here at the store.

130.   Frank - June 10, 1904, Slippery Rock, Pa.

Your welcome letter was received and contents carefully read. Would of answered sooner but lack of time presented. I had thought of waiting until Sun. then write a big epistle but thought I would write a few lines tonight. I have just came from the party 1:30 am. There was a good many there. Amusements were skit and

190

its variations and flinch 2 games and talk. I had rather been writing at this.

I would also like to talk to you but it appears that cannot be at present. As to the date Aug. 25 that was only suggested you have some say in that if you wish.

Money appears to be your only drawback in regard to answering. I am not after your companionship for your money. Money is all right but I have no desire to get a woman for their wealth.

You are the only girl I have had that I cared anything for and I think you agree that I should know what the end result of our friendship should be. I remember that last winter you spoke of wanting to settle down in a home of your own. I am thinking the same thought daily.

I will be happy to receive a favorable reply. You spoke of a sad parting. I see not need of one, but if you still feel that your talents are needed in W.Va. may you have the courage to say <u>no</u>. Then I will be glad to know that I have met you. Happy to know that I never intentionally deceived you and pleased to know that with but few exceptions I always treated you with respect and pleased to know that you are of a good family.

Then last but not least if you decide that my fortune must be as the tramps, I will sincerely wish you well and expect to meet you in heaven.

Martha did not specifically say "No," to his proposal, so Frank has hopes she wants to eventually be with him. It is a matter of timing, not wanting. He must be patient.

You may have picked up on another news item by this time. Belle came home for dinner with Margaret last Sun. and as Jacksville crowd would not take her home, I did. I will be with her next Sun.

eve. at children's day at Harlensburg I expect for the last time. I told her you were coming home soon and could not be with her after that night.

I think Belle recognizes a good catch and would love to start a relationship with Frank. He is being kind to her but is truthful in telling her about Martha.

I was at a party at Moors last Tues. evening, the Hermore crowd, a dozen couples were over. I was partners for Nannie P. Nannie will leave the 9 of next month for the west. I do not expect she will ever be back. Margaret E. got your letter. She going to the S.S. [Sunday School] *and BYPU* [Baptist Young Peoples Union] *convention at Hillsville next week. I am not going this year. Bert was over last Fri. evening and Sat. He started to ride the wheel and the tire played out. He sent for repairs. He talks like as though he was the head man.*

I trust you may not be delayed in answering. If I have said any thing I should not, remember, I wrote this in haste. I always remember you in my prayers and trust you do me. I am anxious for my answer but I don't want you to answer in haste.

CHAPTER 30

QUESTION SETTLED FOR NOW - MAYBE

131.   Martha - June 15, 1904, New Martinsville, W.Va.

I will endeavor to answer your welcome letter which was received Monday. I did not get to answer yesterday. I went out to a little country town to sell a piano. We set the piano in the house but it isn't sold yet. Know [no] use to tell you anything about the trip you do not care enough for W.Va. as that is what you told me once. I seem to like it out hear [here] and probably you would too if you was here to stay any time all I see wrong. We are having some pretty warm weather, just now we had a nice little shower this afternoon which cooled the air of nicely.

I have been all alone in the store today. I gave four music lessons, so I was not idle all the time. I do not know as I care so much for money as you spoke. Money is all right and nice to have but the reason I do not care to go home yet for is because I like my position and have always wanted to be in a place like this and now when I am in it I do not want to give it up yet. The other girl they had in here got her discharge Sat. eve. Mr. Chappelear told me she did not suit him. So it is hard telling when how soon I may get mine. Ha ha. If I do you will see me flying home.

Bert must surly like to stay at the Stone House. You would not of wanted to come and stay that long for the world. Would you?

I have just come back from supper and will try and finish this before any one comes in.

I am glad you enjoyed the party. It is a wonder they didn't play button. Well Frank news is scarce and I can't write as I would talk. I suppose you are thinking she would not talk if she was here.

In his last letter, Frank gives a very complete list of the games they play at a party. Martha had one more in mind and wondered why they didn't play "button." There is an old children's game called Button, button, who's got the button. This could be the game she is referring to but it seems a little childish for these adults.

There was never a word concerning the on-going conversation about the proposal. She is trying to get back to normal about activities in her life in West Virginia.

132.   Frank - June 18, 1904, Slippery Rock, Pa.

Again I write humbly if you were only here I could willing spare more time, but then I suppose I could not <u>behave</u> and you would be leaving me again. I have just come from church at Zion. Eat a large dish of strawberries and a piece of pie. I would have been pleased to of shared them with you, but I suppose you have something better which you would not want to give up.

Ah, this time of year is so famous for Strawberry Festivals, held mostly at churches, even to this day.

Yes I am a Bachelor once more. Had an amusing parting, the Old Mare got after another Odd Fellow and myself. Tell you the particulars later. I expect to remain a bachelor the rest this mo. Hope next mo. will be better.

194

This little bit sounds interesting but we will never know what he meant about the "Old Mare" and the "Odd Fellow." But for sure he is reminding her that he is waiting for her as a bachelor.

I understand Papa was going to see you so I suppose you are exceedingly happy this week. Margaret and Carroll report a fine time at the convention. It will be at Zion next year.

Dear Martha, After I finished writing the above I felt tired and lay down on the bed to rest. When I wakened it was after 5 am.

I am very sorry for I have not much chance to write more today as I am going about 10 mile from here next to Butler to fix a graveyard fence of my grandmother.

I suppose you are very happy now as your Father is no doubt with you by this time.

I only wish I had that pleasure. I called at the Stone House last Sun. and while I would not stay as Bert is doing, yet I would be pleased to stay much more than I do. I took a look in the Parlor, it is still natural. Hope to be there again soon.

It is very nice her father is visiting but Frank is still interested in her family at the Stone House. Apparently Bert is living there. I cannot comment on what their living arrangements were but I haven't seen from these letters that there has been a wedding. I wonder what he means when he says the Parlor is still natural. Maybe he is implying that Bert has not made any changes.

I am real sorry that it was your friend that got discharged.

Nannie Philips is to leave soon and a social gathering is to be there tomorrow eve. as a farewell gathering. There is to be a party at Frank Books on Friday eve. A missionary lecture at Zion Church on Thurs evening and another lecture so on so on by Rev.

Snape of New Castle.

Carroll W. is going to go along to the "Bone Yard" with me. Hope your convention will be a success.

133.   Martha - June 27, 1904, New Martinsville, W.Va.

I will proceed to answer a few of your questions of June 1ˢᵗ and I will also have a few to ask you which I would be glad to have you answer.

There is one thought I have which I want you to think over carefully and then answer and that is, do you think I would be a good help-mate for you on a farm? You know I have spoke I didn't like farm life very well but of course it would be wrong in me to ask you to leave. For your parents need you and would not let you go, although I was always in hopes you would go to town, and was some what disappointed last winter when you came home from N.C. [New Castle] and said you would never be anything but a farmer. I do not dislike the country at all, but I am afraid I would not be strong enough to take the part a wife should take on a farm. Now Frank, I will leave this for you to think over, I just simply mentioned it so I would not disappoint you in after years if such might be the case.

And another one is. Do you think you will ever want to leave the farm some day and go to town?

There is one more which you may think it is a small thing for me to ask but it would be a comfort for me to know and that is, if you would never go to sleep while we were at any gathering?

I will leave these three questions for you to think over carefully and if you can make your answers favorable, mine will be "to what you ask me." but if you wish this letter to be final and do not care to answer them why we can never be any thing more than Friends.

196

And now, we have her answer, well almost. Martha is very concerned about the country life. It has been a topic of conversation many times in these letters and now she can see the outcome is inevitable if she says yes to his proposal. She will be a farmer's wife, and that is obvious, but she is concerned that she might disappoint him. I have to wonder what she was thinking it would be like.

As I sit and recollect my early years visiting the farm, they were very modern. There were cars and tractors outside and they had a television before we had one in our home. Grandma had two big chest freezers on the back porch. Of course I never considered the work it took to fill them. But for sure there was always a piano in their parlor. Even though my recollection is approximately fifty years later, the point is, they stayed modern with the times.

Frank I will not be home for the fourth or I do not think I will be home for a couple months yet. I will stay till my terms of music is out, then I will be home. I think a couple months will finish them.

I will not go home with Papa for he will stop at Pittsburg and I will want to go straight to N.C. [New Castle] when I go. I was certainly glad to see him. He is out to see my brothers now. He will be in this week.

There was a little boy drowned in the river this morning. Him and several other boys were in bathing when he went under. I was very sad. His parents just came home on the nine o'clock train this morning from St. Louis. Was gone a week and he was drowned at ten. They had never seen him yet. That is when they got home. So they never seen him alive again. It was very sad. He was ten years old.

Well Frank it is twelve o'clock and I must get up early in the morning and iron. So I will have to come to a close. I was weighed the eve and I was surprised to think I weighed so much 101 ½ lbs.

I suppose you will think I might of made a better answer but I have concluded to wait and see what you have to say. And if I receive no answer this will mean our parting letter. Now I hope I have not wrote anything to make you feel bad. I haven't wrote any more than I would of ask you in your presence. So do not feel hurt in anything I have said. I will close and look for an early reply if I receive none I will know what your answers were and this will be the last good by. But [be] sure and think the first question over carefully before answering. As ever.

Martha

This ending made me weep as I thought of how difficult it was for her. A young pretty woman, enjoying her life of teaching piano and working at the store, but unsure of her future. She doesn't want to hurt him but must be honest with her feelings. Is she considering all of Frank's qualities that have nothing to do with farming? He is faithful, witty, handsome, intelligent, poetic, giving, a hard worker, and loves the Lord. She doesn't want to disappoint him in the future as not being suited as a country woman. She is asking him to decide.

She goes on, just to make sure he understands where she is coming from. Always the last word.

And another thing, I think you are in to big a hurry to get married. For me, I am in no hurry and do not wish to bind myself down till I am ready. Now of course would not want you to wait on me when there is just as good fish in the sea. I said before I thought I would be home in a month or too. I think it would be foolish to give my scholars up now. I will say no more till I hear from you and if you do not wish to answer send old letters back.

CHAPTER 31

THE ON-GOING PROPOSAL

Frank is tiring of Martha's endless questions. He seems to be getting a bit peevish. He answers her with such detail, obviously putting much thought into the answer. In a way, this can be seen as a very healthy and productive dialog. In today's society these questions are answered simply by living together on a trial basis, not the best idea because there is no commitment. Frank and Martha understand that what they are talking about is for a lifetime. They must be sure.

134.   Frank - June 29, 1904, Slippery Rock, Pa.

Your letter was received today and after reading it carefully several times, I hardly know what to think. Sometimes I think you would be happy if I never wrote again but I cannot hardly believe that, so I write, trusting I did not think right.

When you left you told me you would stay three months and not over four months. Now you speak of staying two or more yet. I do not know much about music terms and as you do not like to leave your students I am sometimes inclined to think there must be some special student that has attractions, that is one of my thoughts sometimes when you speak of staying longer.

199

Last winter I remember of you telling me that you wanted to get settled and have a home of your own. Now you say I am in to big a hurry. I don't just understand it.

I was sorry you said you would not return with your Father. I was expecting to see you and talk with you in person. I do not know whether I can make this answer favorable or not. I will write the truth and pray that the answer will be one which you will never regret.

I am of age and my parents are willing to leave me have my own wish in anything that concerns the future part of my life. I expect to remain a farmer. I did not last year, but now I am happy to belong to a class of people that is master of themselves. True they are not all rich, but they are able to take a vacation when ever they feel like it.

If I am ever fortunate enough as to have a wife, I will expect her to live on the farm with me. For a short time it may be necessary for her to live in this house until another can be built. This in some circumstances would not be advisable but as there is no other heirs to this property to cause trouble, I think it could be done.

At present I do not know what the city could offer me that could be better than I have got. As to the future, I have nothing to say. I cannot predict that. I have had very good success this spring keeping awake and God helping me in the future, I will do the best I can.

Another thing you did not mention which I expect you forgot was the coal bank. I expect to dig some in the future yet not to make a business of it. Yet if it should be necessary I am not ashamed of the dirty hands and face which I get in under the ground.

Again, I always thought you would make me a good companion. If I am so fortunate as to ever get a wife I will expect her to help what she can. But I have never thought of making a slave of her.

I am surprised to know that these questions have troubled you. I thought you had decided about them some time ago yet I am glad you are thinking twice before you decide for the future.

I have written more than you requested yet I tried to do what might be best. If you have any more questions do ask, ask them. I will answer if I can or if you wish to forget me I will return your letters and all else you desire, even the kisses, Haha.

There was a boy, Arn Brandon here a few moments ago to get me to go and help serenade Alice Studebaker and Elmer McComb who was married this evening by Rev. Shoemaker.

Remember If I had any doubts that you were not suited to be a helpmate, I had never asked you and I had ceased to remember you long ago.

If you think I am in to big a hurry about getting married please tell me about when is the proper time that is if you decide to be my consort.

Remember you are young and no doubt have several years to live and I also hope to have the same. And if you think you are not suited to live on a farm better forget me. I don't suppose I will die of grief.

I expect an answer soon for I know if this letter is not favorable you will hasten to say <u>farewell</u> and if it is favorable you will be pleased to tell me that I may be.

Frank is still signing "Your Hubby" But it is very important to watch the dates of the letters because some crossed in the mail. Martha writes the following before she see the one above.

135.   Martha - July 1, 1904, New Martinsville, W.Va.

I am going to write you a few lines this morning in correction of my last letter which no doubt you have read by this time. I was so busy at the time I wrote the other letter that my mind was all unsettled. We was getting ready for the convention and I was up every night till late and then try to write a letter in the store is no fun. So I hardly know what I did write and I was afraid there was some things in it that you would misunderstand me. Meby [sic] I did not write them as I meant too. So to give you a clear understanding I am writing this and hope it is not to late. I am going to give you my full answer this morning and then you answer the questions I have ask you.

Martha did not receive Frank's lengthy letter of June 29 as of this writing. She is making excuses for her letter of June 27, where she asked the three questions for him to answer. She must be thinking that she wrote some things she should not have written. Frank's original proposal was a month ago and she needs to give him an answer.

I am sorry to of kept you waiting so long but you have certainly been patient: but I think there will be happiness at the end.

The question you ask me in Jun 1st letter the answer is (Yes). If you think I can make you a good wife on a farm I am willing to go with you and hope we shall be happy together.

Now Frank, I would be glad to have you answer them questions I ask. No doubt you will think this was funny way to do but there is always sorrow before happiness.

Well it is time to go to the store and must close and yes I want to say I would like to stay these two months and finish my scholars but I will do as you say. I would like very much to see you too. I think while I am here I would like to finish these terms of music.

136.   Frank - July 3, 1904, Slippery Rock, Pa.

On last evening I was so completely surprised that I do not feel capable of showing my appreciation of the honor you have bestowed upon me.

I was not expecting a reply to my letter until about Wed. and I had not much idea it would contain much good news. I did not feel the best. My mind was unsettled. My plans for the future dark. And you can imagine my surprise when I came to supper to receive a letter from you. I did not even dare to guess the contents the two letters are so unlike that I think something must have happened to of prompted you to write.

I most certainly appreciate your answer and I hope you may never regret it.

I would be as pleased to see you as you would be to see me but harvest is now here and I do not think it would be wise to me to go. So I think we can wait until you have finished your terms for a you desire I am willing for you to remain theses two months more.

It is settled with her definite YES and Frank is willing to wait two more months for her return. He is contented, he finally has the answer he waited for.

I am going to spend part of the fourth with John Dambaugh at Cascade. My plans were different until I got your letter then I was pleased to change them as they had not been exposed to any one else.

Some interesting fact about Cascade Park: "Originally known as Big Run Falls, the site was purchased in 1892 by Col. Levi Brinton. Around the turn of the century, power companies were finding it profitable to develop amusement parks. In 1897 Col. Brinton sold the property to New Castle Traction Co., which later became Pennsylvania Power Company. After extensive landscaping and addition of numerous rides, the company held a contest to name the park. In deference to its cascading waterfall, it became known as Cascade Park. Cascade Park opened May 29, 1897. Cascade Park soon became a popular excursion point from much of western Pennsylvania and eastern Ohio. Special excursion trains would arrive in New Castle on East Washington Street and streetcars would carry passengers to the Park. Up to 7,200 people could be transported daily to the Park. The company built a theater, a baseball park, a roller coaster, and installed a merry-go-round. The company built the largest dance pavilion, which is still standing, in Pennsylvania in 1898, lighted with 45 arc lights. A lake for boating, swimming and skating, as well as a zoo and a picnic grove, were added the following year."[27]

Those questions I answered before I got your letter and I am glad I did. I am also glad you answered before you received it. It is certainly a funny way of doing but there I appreciate it all the same.

Ha, he realizes it is a good thing she answered before she had to letter of June 29 in her hands. He knows his sweetheart oh so well.

---

[27]visitlawrencecounty.com

CHAPTER 32

HURT FEELINGS

137.   Martha - July 8, 1904, New Martinsville, W.Va.

Martha is now responding to the letter of the 29th. She admits how sad it made her. The trials and tribulations of this long proposal are on-going.

I will endeavor to write you a few lines. No doubt you will think I am a good while about answering but I could not help it. I have been so down hearted and mind unsettled since I received your letter of June 29th that I could not sit down to write. I was very much disappointed in that letter. The reason I wrote my last letter when I did is because I had waited for an answer and I had begun to think you was not going to answer and I had guessed at the answers by which I heard you say, but some of them was so much different than I expected and then you spoke of things I never heard you speak of before. And which would mean a great deal to me that I feel we could not agree on. But I will be willing to leave it stand as it is till I come home and we can have a better understanding. I will be home just as soon as I get through with my terms.

Martha is upset and is rambling on and on. But she concedes to leave things as written previously.

I suppose you are beginning to think before this that I am a very funny girl no doubt you will think right. Still it is a hard matter to understand miles apart. I suppose you think I might come home. But I told you why I was staying.

Now I do not mean to write this to make you feel bad but I thought you ought to know how I was feeling over your letter and that is why I write this. I was certainly disappointed. But probably I didn't understand some things as you meant them. So if you are willing let us correspond as we always have done till I come home. You have my answer and if we can agree on all things then it will stand and if not why if will half to go other wise.

Frank's long letter of the 29th was very unsettling to her. It is a good thing that she had already given him her answer. The many miles between them is taking a toll on their relationship. She just does not see these things as he does. A little change of subject follows.

We have a carnival here this week. We have had some great times. It closes today. This is an awful warm day. Well Frank the man that owns the store wants the ink so I will close for this time hoping this finds you well. I shall look for an answer soon.

138.   Frank - July 12, 1904, Slippery Rock, Pa.

Franks starts this letter out with"Dear Friend." I would think after the previous letter where she said yes, he would not be so formal.

I am sorry my last letter did not suit you and as I answered by return mail a thing which you scarcely even do I got the reply to you as quick as I could and as that is not soon enough for you I wonder what I think when you take 3 or four days to answer.

I guess you will have to take me on trial such as Mae appears to be doing with Bert. I don't know whether he is still there or not but suppose he is.

I will say no more on the subject for some time. You are to far away to reason with and I am an Odd Fellow. No wonder your mind is unsettled, taking the pleasure of leap year away from you.

Finally, some small talk—no more proposal.

I had a very good time at Cascade. The rain spoiled the fireworks. It has rained every day since and a good many before. I sent you a letter that day which I suppose you got.

Margaret and Roy got lost coming home, drove into town and their horse scared and drove them to the curbstone and smashed the wheel and cross bars. They got a few bruises, nothing serious.

Rev. Snape of New Castle Baptist church lectured at Zion last Fri. Evening on How to find yourself. It was very good.

I am invited to the wedding through Margaret as yet of my first girl Sadie Weimer on the 18th of Aug. I would like to see her and ask her if she and Otto ever doubted their suitability to each other.

I had thought of giving you some reveries of a Batchelor but have not time. Margaret wants me to cut weeds.

I want to tell you I enjoy my drive these fine Sunday evenings. Mable book is 19 tomorrow evening so when you are reading this I expect to be with a few others calling on her.

139.   Martha - July 18, 1904, New Martinsville, W.Va.

I will endeavor to answer your most welcome letter which was received. I intended to answer last night after I came from church but I had the headache so bad I went to bed instead. I am sorry you will not receive an answer any sooner but I will try to any way. I am not kicking that you don't write soon enough. You do remarkably well and it makes me think that much more of you.

I am real sorry that I cause you so many disappointments but you have such pleasant Sunday evenings that will soon wear off the disappointments I cause you. I have about come to think I had better stay out here. If I where to go home I would meby cause you to break those pleasant times.

Martha just doesn't want to hear that Frank is enjoying himself. Even after she said yes to his proposal, she still writes of insecurities. She maybe should stay in West Virginia so she won't disappoint him. This long distance relationship is so difficult.

I have been having some good times too. There was seventeen of us went out for a hay ride one evening last week. We certainly had a good time and made a lot of music. They got a lot of horns and we sang all the songs we new [knew]. We went out two miles out of town and then on all the streets in town there was a wagon full of us and we thorough [sic] hay all over each other. After that we went to one of the girls homes and had sherbet and cake. Meby you never eat any of that but it is another kind of ice cream and it was fine too. I suppose you get enough hay ride without taking them that way. Have you begun to harvest yet? But it is a treat for us city people. Ha, Ha.

It has been raining very hard. The water is standing in pools but it is just fine it has cooled the air of nicely. They say yesterday was the hottest day there has been yet this summer.

Father is safely home again I had a card from them. He thinks a good bit of his farm since he seen these hills of W.Va. He enjoyed his trip very much. Charlie, wife, Harry, and Father was all here for the fourth. There was an awful crowd in town that day but there was not much going on. There was a carnival here but it was not

very much. The rain spoiled the fireworks also.
I am glad you had a good time. I received that letter you sent on that day. I also received the <u>heart</u>. Did you mean that for your heart? Ha, Ha.

CHAPTER 33

BACK TO NORMAL

140.   Frank - July 22, 1904, Slippery Rock, Pa.

Since I received your epistle I have been exceedingly busy. Harvest is now on so with my night work I must put necessity before pleasure.

On the day I mailed you my last letter I received a special invitation to that wedding. I was working corn today in the a.m. and in the hay in p.m. I have plenty of hay rides now. Have no need of taking the old wagon with some hay over the country to see the beauty of nature with a choice crowd. There might be pleasure enough but for me, give me a sweet country maiden and an old buckboard and a horse that needs no driving and I will try and be contented.

Frank is back to his sweet old self, saying such lovely things to Martha.

I was at a party at Blanche and Olive Studebaker's Wed. eve. Will Rolland is working for us now on Mon. eve. after leaving the hay field I challenged him to go to call on Olive and a Miss Nell Sherman of New Castle. We went with our old clothes, did not fix

210

up any. I heard the piano for the first time since Feb. In leaving they told us to bring our sister down. Wed. eve. I sent Margaret on ahead and I went about 9:30 to a bring her home. But was exceedingly surprised to find several others there all fixed up in style. I had my old clothes on again but I did not go home for all I was the Bum. I did not go to sleep either.

I spent yesterday at the Wayside Inn at Grove City. If you take a Pittsburg paper you will know the particulars the crowd was estimated at 3000 however the crowd though immense would not reach that amount. Mabelle B. was my partner for the day she was not well in the afternoon so did not enjoy it as well as I would of like to of had her do. She is all right today. I met Victor there I did not know him at first and as I had my lodge badge on he had a little or no trouble in naming me although he was not sure at first.

Grove City has not been mentioned in theses epistles as of yet. It is a lovely town about seven miles north of Slippery Rock, Pa. There is a very good college located there and many interesting shopping destinations as well.

Apparently the gathering had to do with the Odd Fellows lodge Frank belonged to. "The Wayside Inn was the forerunner of Orchard Manor, Inc. It was built by the Independent Order of Odd Fellows for Brothers of the Fellowship and their widows. The establishment of the home was recommended by the lodges of Western Pennsylvania on January 10, 1901. In the following May it was approved by the grand lodge, and the institution was incorporated July 18, 1901. The location of the home was selected from twenty- two possible sites in November."[28]

141.   Martha - July 29, 1904, New Martinsville, W.Va.

I suppose you are kept very busy now when harvest is on. Do you

---

[28]Grovecityhistoricalsociety.org

have very much fruit this year. I bet I had something for dinner yesterday you haven't had yet and that was corn on the cob. It was pretty good for the first. Do you still have your appetite yet?

There is one of my chums, remember girl friends, is going to leave here Monday to visit out in that direction. She goes to Oil City and handy Butler. We have in view a boat ride tomorrow eve before she leaves. I don't now [sic] whether we will get it or not. The river is very low now. There isn't only one or two big boats running now. The rest are all tied up. I meant we was going to take a skiff ride. I have had one ride there was several of us got a skiff one evening. I think it is fine. I learnt how to row, the other girls know how.

What has become of Sam P? You never say anything about him. I just wondered if he was at home this summer.

I forgot to tell you in the last letter that I got that picture too. It was very good of you. Only I thought you looked awful poor. I presume you are working to hard this hot weather but I guess you can only make hay when the sun shines. So I suppose it has to be done. I presume you are looking forward to the time when Miss Martin comes to visit you. That will be nice. I hope you have a pleasant visit together.

142.   Frank - Aug.1, 1904, Slippery Rock, Pa.

I received your welcome letter today. It has been about two weeks since you wrote and I had many thoughts about that girl. Among them these, is she sick? Did she not receive my letter? Is she not pleased about something I wrote? Or has she grown tired of me and by waiting a few times is going to let me down easy? Perhaps such thoughts are foolish, but never the less they come. This letter will be full of complaints. You say I looked poor in the picture if I am it is <u>worry</u> not work that makes me so.

We have about 7 loads of hay to put up yet. Then comes the oats. We have not a large crop of apples this year, will have several peaches and a nice amount of plumbs. Have not had any corn yet but will have soon.

Sam P.? Is working at Books near Hermon church. He and Jim still goes steady to VanHorns. I do not see him very often.

You misunderstand about Miss Martin. She is not coming on purpose to see me, but Nora Dambaugh, however I would not be much surprised if she would not come as school will soon begin.

Bert is here this evening. He has told Mother and Margaret that he is to be married soon. Mame [Martha's sister] is out helping to sew. He has not told me yet, but said he was going the last of this week to look for a farm near town. I have just given him your letter to read. His opinion is this. A very nice friendly letter but would expect more from one when we were so well acquainted.

He tells me you are now talking of not coming home until in Sept. I trust it is not to be so. I was expecting to hear of your being in town last Sun. But was disappointed. If I have to I can wait the rest of that time but if you wish to be better acquainted don't disappoint me to often. It's a game I don't like. You say you have some plans which you would like to work out. I have some too but I can't work them until I know some of yours.

As we see, Frank is so anxious and it must have been so disappointing to hear such news from someone else. He accuses her of "playing games" with him.

Miss Gertrude Ryan of New Brighton talked to the B.Y.P.U. on the national convention held at Detroit this year. Communion is next Sabbath.

Patterson reunion is the 10th of this month. Would be pleased to

213

have you there. Shall I meet you?

This letter I expect will not please you but remember, I have held myself about as long as I can. To understand me better you must be nearer. Mistakes are not hay stacks or you would get rich from this epistle.

P.S. After I finished the above, Bert told me of good fortune. I will say no more for I suppose you know more than I do as he says you have known of it for sometime. I am painting our old buggy today. We are all well. Hope you are also. Remember me to the Black family. Trusting you will favor me with an early reply this time and I will try an not complain again. Don't censure me to severely. I am or suppose I may still say,

Your Hubby

Frank

CHAPTER 34

TRIP TO THE OIL FIELDS

143.   Martha - *Aug 4, 1904, Dulaney, W.Va.*

If you can excuse my lead pencil I will answer your letter which I received last night. It read so much different than some of your last letters that I will answer it right away and not make it two weeks this time as you said I did before but I do not believe it was that long. I am way out in the oil fields this afternoon. I am writing this letter in a tent. We all came out to where Mr. Black is working. We started early this morning and drove about seventeen miles and the roads is not like they are out there. I got pretty tired but will try and answer your letter for it takes it longer to go. We intend to stay out here till Sunday. Mr. Black's brother lives here so that is where we are staying. I just wish you could see the country. The hills is just straight up and they drill the wells on them hills. I don't see how they get the tools up to where the well is.

I love how she describes the mountains of West Virginia. I looked on the map to find Dulaney. As I looked at the access from New Martinsville to Dulaney, the roads form a switchback. It is not clear whether she was in an automobile or carriage. I can remember many years ago riding in our car through these mountains and feeling like Martha.

215

Frank I am sorry you have so much to worry about that it has made you poor. I hope you will be more cheerful when that letter reaches you. I don't know whether I will have very much in it to cheer you up any but I will try to. I am sorry I disappointed you last Sun. How does it come you thought I would be in town or New Castle. I never wrote you anything to that effect. It may be several Sundays yet? There I am writing something again to disappoint you but hope not. I want to be here for the fair and then I am going to visit my brothers a couple weeks and then I may go home. For if things are as you said Bert said I will be needed at home. Yes I have known it - but Mae did not want me to say anything so that is the reason I never told you. I thought you would find it out sooner or later. I don't know very much about it only they are going to get married.

I did not know Mame was out there sewing. Is she out there now? I would of liked very much to of been out there for the reunion and am sorry I can't be but hope you have a nice time. Where is it to be held this year? Never mind. I will be home some of these times and may come unexpected. Then you will be sorry I came for you will just half to make those trips over in Law. Co. again and lose a lot of sleep where you can get all the sleep you want now.

I also remember that you said in one of your letters that if we quit you would not die of grief. I took a great deal of meaning from that but will not say any thing more now and wait for a more convenient time.

When I read this in the letter of June 29th I thought Martha would have a good deal to say. However in her response of July 8th she doesn't mention it then, but she didn't forget.

I really have the headache so bad I can hardly hold my head up so if there is any thing in the letter that don't please you consider the source. I don't know whether I have spelled all the words right or not. If I haven't pass them over. I hope you will write something that didn't please me your last letter was all right if there was a little more of it. Still it was a pretty good sized letter and I enjoyed reading it.

Well as it is about suppertime and I did want to write Mame a few lines yet but I don't know whether my head will allow me or not. I guess I have written all I can think of for this time and hope it will reach you in good time. I of course could have more to say if you were here but I have written all I want to say in this way. I can not say at the present time when I will be home but I may go at any time. I could not say as I have said before I may come unexpected.

144.   Frank - Aug.7, 1904, Slippery Rock, Pa.

The first page of this letter is written "between the lines" similar to the April Fool's letter.

I was agreeably surprised yesterday to receive your letter. If I thought another cranky letter would bring as quick a reply I would mix some complaints but I trust you will answer promptly. There was a very good attendance at church today.

Oats harvest is here now. I swing the cradle yesterday for the first. I also had corn on the cob and as I still have my good appetite I enjoyed it very much. The reunion is to be held at uncle Smith Patterson near North Liberty this year. There will be a picnic at Zion Church of the S.S. [Sunday School] on 18 of this month. I do not expect to be present as I go to Ohio that day if nothing prevents.

In your letter you said you took a great deal of meaning about me not going to "Dye" of grief. To understand what I meant you will have to be nearer as it would take to long to write it in full.

Frank underlined, twice, and had quotation marks and spelled it as dye. We will never know what he meant but it sounds like he is trying to down play the words.

Where is the Fair you wish to attend?

I don't know where Mame is now. I am exceedingly troubled about going to Law. Co. again. I am going over some of the these days soon so as to get used to it before the rush comes. I will be exceedingly surprised to hear of you being in New Castle. No difference when you come, as I have learned to my sorrow that your promises about coming home, at least are about as good as though that were written on ice. They are liable to change.

Sun eve.
My best girl and I were at Mt. Union tonight. She has been wanting to go for a long time. This was their Communion evening, the church was very much crowded. Sam and Jim had their best girls there also.

Perhaps I had better tell you who my girl was or you will decide to remain until after after Xmas. It was one who loves me more than you or any one else is likely to do for a while even though she may not often say. It was my mother. She appeared pleased to have you remember her. Do you still work at the store? Tell me all about yourself. If you can spare the time answer promptly. Frank

It is sweet that he calls his mother his "best girl." Not just that, but he is willing to take her where she wants to go. No "Your Hubby" on this letter. Now he adds another thought and as the page is full, he writes around the sides.

You will get this Tues. eve and in two days after I look for a reply. I weigh 155 #. I am getting bald headed.

Now the next day, Monday, he adds more. Rather than starting a new page, he writes between the lines of page one. Never in one letter has Martha or Frank turned the page over and written on the back.

Mon. I am binding oats today. I don't work very hard. Never did. Don't know how. Better not read anymore. Don't read between the lines. There is more I have not written than I have. Hope your head has quit hurting. Come to me and I will hold your head. I ... girl you will look on the other pages to see if there are all like this is. Excuse mistakes. Your farmer friend. My paper is scared I guess I will have to get another supply. I am going to feed my pigs now. I have 13 in all – more coming. Good bye F.V.P.

145.   Martha - Aug. 15, 1904, New Martinsville, W.Va.

I will try and write you a few lines this afternoon. Sorry I did not get to answer sooner but thought I would wait and give you a chance to get a writing tablet. I think your paper was scarce, the next time you write like that I won't answer for a couple weeks. But trust you was not dissappointed [sic] any when you did not get a letter last week. You said you was use to dissappointments [sic] so I suppose you would not care much.

Ha, Martha doesn't like his skimping on the paper just as she didn't like his letter in April.

Last week was a very full week and this week is going to be the same. We got home from the oil field last Monday evening and I was glad to get back. It is a very rough country. They have know [sic] more regard for Sunday than any other day. I do not mean they are all that way but the majority. I do not think I care to go again for some time although I had a right good time. We all had our pictures taken in a group and they are a peach. I was not out there hardly a day till there was a young man I had never met him but he ask Mr. Black to ask me if I would go with him to the dance that eve. They had a dance at the boarding house. But what do you think of that? I guess you know my opinion on <u>dance</u>. I did not hear the last of that while I was out there.

219

Yesterday I went out to call on one of my girlfriends just across the street. They moved up in this corner last week. This man that moved up here is a very wealthy man. And this girl is there niece she has been here since May. This man has a half interest in a yacht so they all took a notion we would take a yacht ride. We was out on the river about an hour. It was my first ride in a yacht. There was just him and his family and this girl and I but we enjoyed it.

Martha has been enjoying boating on the Ohio River since she has been in New Martinsville. There is nothing like it where she is going in Pennsylvania. It has been a great experience for this young lady.

We are going to have our Sunday School Picnic next Wednesday at VanCamps Grove. We go on the street cars to the place. We expect to take dinner and supper there so we will half to go with well filled baskets. I guess I had better cease writing about having so many good times or you will think that is all I do. But they just come when there nothing else on hand. I suppose you are contemplating on going to see your old sweetheart married. I hope you have a pleasant trip.

CHAPTER 35

SHORT BUT SWEET

146.   Frank - Aug.17, 1904, Slippery Rock Pa.

This letter came in an envelope with a poem printed on it as follows:

PREPARE TO MEET THY GOD
          ****

Vain man, thy fond pursuits forebear;
Repent, thine end is nigh;
Death, at the farthest, can't be far:
O think before thou die.

Reflect, thou hast a soul to save;
Thy sins, how high they mount!
What are thy hopes beyond the grave?
How stands the dark account?

Death enters, and there's no defense;
His time there's none can tell;
He'll in a moment call thee hence,
To heaven, or down to hell.

Thy flesh, perhaps thy greatest care,
Shall into dust consume;
But ah! destruction stops not there;
Sin kills beyond the tomb.
          ****
Short Sermon Series, No. 5. 30c per 100

ADVOCATE Office, Fort Scott, Kans.

Your letter came in time to save me giving the mail carrier --- a little good advice. He has miscarried some of our mail twice and the third will cause trouble. However the substitute carrier will not carry long.

While I am used to dissapointments [sic] yet it does not make me appreciate the giver any more for it. However I suppose I am to much of a crank anyway.

Harvest days will soon be over. I am contemplating going to Ohio tomorrow.

PS Don't put yourself to any extra trouble to answer. I'll try and wait also. I send a message on the envelope to some stranger whom chance to read. Hope it won't offend you. Farmer F.V.P

147.   Martha - Aug. 22, 1904, New Martinsville, W.Va.

I am very sorry for dissappointing you so many times and hope you will forgive me. I am going to have some good news for you in one of my letters soon. I am going out to visit Charlie and Harry Friday. I do not know how long I will be gone. I don't think any longer than a week and then going <u>Home.</u>

I am not in the store now and my terms are about all out. So you will hear of me being in New Castle one of these days.

I had a fine time at our S.S. Picnic. I was not worth very much the next day.

I presume you are home from your visit to Ohio.

Well Frank I haven't much to write this time I will be glad when we won't have to write. And all that I know now I expect to see you before many days hence.

Now I will close and go and try and finish up some fancy work I have started for Laura. So good bye for this time. I will look for an <u>*early reply*</u> *and a much larger letter than the last. Hoping you are well. I am (As Ever) Martha*

148.   Frank - Aug.24, 1904, Slippery Rock, Pa.

Your welcome note was received today and I will try and answer although I may have to kick myself two or more times to make sure I am not dreaming.

I am surprised (?) to know your thoughts turn home and will indeed be surprised to see you. I am anxiously awaiting the summons to come. But then thoughts come. How long can you be contented in the country? How soon until you wish to return to your class? And then there will be such a nice class 10 or12 ready to start at once also Laura wants me etc...

And another reverie. What about Frank? Will he be what you expect him to be after 6 mo. and more absence? And what well he expect? I'd rather guess than tell.

Frank is excited that she said she will be home soon but can't believe it. He is dredging up all the insecurities of the past and doubting himself. Now that it is closer to being reality, he is wondering if it will be good enough.

I was hauling oats today, rain has kept us back. If tomorrow is nice we will finish and then plowing. We have started the plow. I got home from the wedding O.K. Did not feel very good for a few days, am better now. It was Dutch over 150 near 200 guests many fine presents. Will say more when you are present.

Hope these few lines finds you well. I must close and go to sleep. I could talk more if you were present. Remember me to your Bro's. Bert is in New Castle in furniture store now salesman.

I am anxiously awaiting your coming.
Your Hubby.

CHAPTER 36

ALMOST HOME

149.   Martha - Sept. 2, 1904, New Martinsville, W.Va.

I suppose you have looked for a letter before this time But all the excuse I have is I just neglected to write. I just came in from my Bro's on the one o'clock train. I have an awful headache but I had a real nice time out there. Will not take time to tell you. I will wait till I see you then I can tell you better the sights I saw.

I had a notion not to write till I get to New Castle but thought I would drop you a few lines anyway, and then I would drop you a line from N.C. And if it won't be to much trouble to come in after me, I would be pleased to have you come. And if you could not come have a letter for me in N.C. when I get there.

I expect to leave here about Wed. or Thurs, if nothing happens but I want to stay in N.C. a couple days. Well I guess I will not write any more this time as I can talk better when I see you and will drop you a line from N.C.

150.   Martha - Sept. 8, 1904, New Martinsville, W.Va.

I told you in the other letter that I would write from N.C. But as I will not start from here till tomorrow morning I would not have time to write from there so you may come in for me Sunday if you can. I am packing my trunk now so will write know[sic] more. Hoping to see you soon.

151.   Frank - Sept. 8, 1904, Slippery Rock, Pa.

Since taking to Mame Tues. I find I may not be able to get to go to town Friday or Sat morning so I will go Sun. if you do not leave other directions at W.E. Patterson grocery for me in care of J.C. Patterson on Sat before 3 o'clock. Will explain more fully when we meet. Yours, Frank
Am sorry to dissapoint you.

CHAPTER 37

HOME IN PENNSYLVANIA

152.   Martha - Sept. 10 1904, New Castle, Pa. The envelope says "In care of J.C. Patterson" as instructed above. There is no postage on the envelope.

I just received your letter and as you can't come in for me today [Saturday] and Bert is going out this afternoon I will just go out with him and save you the trip. I arrived in New Castle yesterday and as I know I am needed at home I will just go out this afternoon.

I suppose you will be over soon. So will say no more for this time.

There are no more letters until April 1905. Frank and Martha are together. All the things Frank had been dreaming about are coming true and Martha is getting used to country life. I imagine there were many parties and church functions to attend as a couple. They certainly were able to have Christmas together with all the festivities. They can now have a grand time in a real courtship, planning their future together.

153.   Frank – April 7, 1905, Slippery Rock, Pa.

My mother had a note on the front of this envelope stating, "I believe Martha was looking for a seamstress to make her wedding dress."

I got home O.K. Last eve about 10 o'clock. I met Ida R. and Nannie White walking so did not get this # neither can she come to your place to sew now. Hope you have good luck finding one in N.C. And if you can't find one you might get my cousin Nannie Patterson. 20 Allen St. She is good so at least has had lots of experience in fine sewing. The only drawback is you have to speak to her in writing. I was plowing today. Margaret was much surprised. Ida and Nannie promised not to blow up my message. Hope you are well.

Let me know your progress. Frank

154.   Martha - This letter has no dates or a stamp. It is just a short letter to Frank.

My dear Frank,
I just got your letter. Am sorry I could not get her but I will try in here. I do not know what success I will have.

I will let you know later when to come in after me. Well as May and Sade is ready to go down street with me I will have to close. I am not near through shopping yet, if I can't get a dress maker I suppose I will let you know pretty soon. Hoping you are well.
I am yours,
Martha XX - There is the one you did not get.

Ah ha, Martha is in love. This is first letter she starts with, "My dear Frank." And she ends with kisses. Love and wedding activities are in the air. She is going shopping with her sisters. What fun it must have been for her. New Castle was a bustling city then with many stores. They probably visited all of them.

155.   Martha - Apr. 12, 1905, New Castle, Pa.

April 12 was Wednesday so she is giving him plenty of time to plan to bring her home on the weekend. The last letter is making arrangements to be together.

I will drop you a few lines this evening to let you know when you can come in after me, if it will be convenient for you. I am getting anxious to get home and also to see you. I can be ready to go home by Friday evening if you get this letter in time. I did not know that I would be ready to go at that time till this evening.

I will write I think you will get it before that time. I knew it would not be very convenient for you Sat evening, unless you prefer that evening, but come one of those evenings, Fri eve. if possible so I can help Ma with the Saturday work.

But come to go home after dark because if you din't [sic] there will be a story going.
Well I will leave the rest of the news till I see you and close
Hoping you are well.
I remain your, Martha

THE END

But it isn't. The letters are finished but their life together was just beginning. The last letter was dated April 12, 1905 and they were married on April 26, 1905. Frank and Martha began a bond, a triangle of love with one another and with the Lord Jesus at the top of the triangle.

The Bible says in Isaiah 62:5, "For as a young man marries a young woman, so shall your sons marry you, and as the bridegroom rejoices over the bride, so shall your God rejoice over you."

A wedding is a wonderful time of excitement for everyone. Weddings in this century are quite different than that of Frank and Martha. There are many parties involved - often trips out of town to exotic destinations for bachelor and bachelorette parties, parties to select the dress, and of course the wedding shower. All culminating in a great and glorious reception with food, music and dancing. A huge celebration for sure. Sad to say, some of these weddings are all about the parties with no mention of God blessing their union.

There is another wedding celebration talked about in the Bible. Revelation 19:7–8 says,
"Let us rejoice and exult and give him the glory, for the marriage of the Lamb has come, and his Bride has made herself ready; it was granted her to clothe herself with fine linen, bright and pure— for the fine linen is the righteous deeds of the saints."

Jesus Christ is the Bridegroom and the church, believers in Christ, are the bride. This wedding takes place in heaven at the end of time.

This shows us a beautiful picture of love. Christ loves everyone and wants to have a relationship with them. Just as when a couple is married, they become one, so believers are one with Christ.

Frank and Martha had this relationship with the Lord as we saw many times in the letters. Even though at times there seemed doubts, and some hard feelings, in the end, they always wanted the Lord's will to determine the outcome in their lives.

Indeed, they were blessed as they continued to live their life with the Lord as the head of their home.

Frank at his desk

Martha in front of Zion Church

EPILOGUE

On April 26, 1955 there was another celebration. It was Frank and Martha's 50th Wedding Anniversary. I can still remember it even though I was not yet 10 years old. In the preface, I mentioned that it was my mother who saved the letters and handed them down to me. Mom was sentimental and loved to celebrate and wanted a big celebration for her parent's 50th.

The planning was complete and the party started. There was a lovely dinner at the Harlensburg Inn, then the family came back to the Patterson home for a program mom had put together. The handsome couple renewed their vows with my father officiating. Then the children performed for their grandparents. My cousin played the Grand Steel guitar, my two brothers played what was called a tonet which they had learned in school. It was like a flute. They played a Stephen Foster song that Granddad liked called, "Old Black Joe." I did what was called a musical reading. My mother played the piano and I recited a poem called "Chester Jenkins." The finale was my mom reading a poem she had written to honor her parents.

Three Cheers for Fifty Years

Listen, Dear Folks, and you shall hear
Of the Mom and Pop we love so dear.
'Twas the twenty-sixth of April in nineteen five--
None of us children were then alive
To witness that famous day and year.
But this is what happened, we do surmise,
to Frank and Martha whom we idolize.

Young Frank hitched the mare to the one-hoss shay
As he thought of this—his one great day.
Over the hill—not too far to ride--
Was waiting a sweet young thing—his bride.
Soon he would waft her away so fast
From her Ma and Pa, whom he had ask'd,
And wave good-bye just as they passed.

The mare galloped along and loud did neigh
For even she knew 'twas a wedding day.
To New Castle town—fifteen miles to go--
The horse was neither lazy or slow.
The groom in his derby, the bride in her suit,
Where smiling and gay and sure did look cute.

First to the court house the license to get,
Then off to the parsonage. Excited? You bet!!
The preacher was waiting with book in hand
Though knees did quiver and almost shake,
They loved each other--'twas no mistake.

"Do you take this woman to be your wife?"
Frank almost answered, "You bet your life."
But caught himself, "I do," he cried.
No happier words could he say if he'd tried.
"Will you love, cherish, honor, and try to obey?"
To this he answered, "I'll do as you say."

To Martha the Parson then turned with a smile
And asked her the question she's pondered a while,
"Do you take for your husband this eager young man?"
To which her heart whispered, "That's been my plan."
But she uttered, "I do," as she gazed in Frank's eyes.
She knew from that moment she's won a grand prize.

And after the words make them husband and wife,
There began from that moment a blest wedded life.
Frank took from his pocket a five dollar bill
And paid the preacher so there'd be no ill will.
The mare had been patient and full of pride
As she waited outside for the knot to tied.

After the service, past ten by the clock,
They started, it's true, a new life to unlock.
They stabled the mare and a cab did hail.
Off to the train-- they would go by rail
On their honeymoon, which is just the thing
For a bride and groom in the time of Spring.

Niagara Falls was one of their goals,
And all could see they were happy souls.

Away for a week to see the sights
Busy they were for days and nights.

Back home at last on the Patterson Farms
He took her, whenever he wished, in his arms.
She mended his socks and cooked his stew,
And did all the things a good wife should do.
He fed the pigs and milked the cows
And always glad he took the vows.

On October the 20th in 1906
The topic discussed was not just chicks.
A boy named Kenneth became the first heir.
He took the attention of the happy pair.
By the dresses he wore, hair ribbon, and curl,
One would have thought they'd wanted a girl.

Two years hence on a September night
A cry was heard with great delight.
Cecil Jess had come to stay
With whom his brother Ken could play.

Boys are a help, indeed, on the farm,
But what about a little charm?
So again in 1910 they found a bright September pearl
When the Doc turned to Frank and said, "It's a girl!"
It took this babe named Thelma Grace
To keep them all at a rapid pace.

All five in the family got along fine
Until one day they heard a new whine.
'Twas the month of February in the year fifteen
A new little sister appeared on the scene.
They thought at first she'd rule as Queen!
She kept them up nights, much attention she claimed,
More food she needed—they should be ashamed.

Although for two weeks she was hungry and mad,
They had high hopes and named her Glad.

Two years later in December cold
Johnny boy was dear to hold.
So sweet and happy, with rolls of fat,
How pleased they were with this last little Pat.
"Our family's here and that's no bluff."
They both thought Five were quite enough.

There were washings and ironings and jobs galore,
All too often a spill on the floor.
Married life was indeed full of thrills
With babies and bottles, and Oh! the bills!

Now memories of those years pass in review--
There was school, and work, and romance too,
College and weddings, and John off to War
To spend three years in the Army Corps.

From the time Dan Cupid first shot his dart
Frank and Martha stayed young at heart.
Tho' it was kids and work of many a kind
they never refused to help mankind.

All through the years it was do this and that;
There were only a few times when they really Just Sat!
If it wasn't Church, it was W.C.T.U.
Then there was Grange and Politics too.

Many a Sunday and week day fine
Friends and relatives on chicken did dine.
Off to the Farm, a day to spend,
Of eating and talking there seemed no end.

The eight grandchildren think an awful lot

Of the Grandma and Granddad that they have got.
They love to be on the farm to stay
To eat, and sleep, work some, and play.

Often much laughter and even some tears
Were bound to be found down thru the years,
When some of the loved ones and friends they knew
Quietly and quickly from this life withdrew.

We thank the Lord in Heaven Above
For parents with such unselfish love,
Who cuddled us and spanked our rears
And guided us through all these years.
God gives the health and the strength they need
That still today many others they lead.

And now, dear Ones, we celebrate
This Fiftieth Anniversary date.
To Frank and Martha, husband and wife,
We give three cheers for a long wedded life.

By Gladys Patterson Taylor April 26, 1955

Frank and Martha lived a full life five years beyond this celebration. Granddad went home to be with the Lord on August, 1960. Just as these two lived together here on earth, the Lord thought it fitting to take Grandma home two weeks later.

Frank and Martha at Niagara Falls on their honeymoon.

Martha and Frank's last photograph together.

ABOUT THE AUTHOR

Nancy McClintock lives in Florida where she and her late husband, Frank, moved from Pittsburgh, Pennsylvania in 2014. She has two sons and two stepdaughters. She also has seven grandchildren and one great granddaughter. Nancy spent over thirty years working as a nurse, most recently as the manager of an outpatient surgery center before retiring in 2008. Her favorite calling in life is teaching the Bible. She has led numerous Bible studies over many years. She believes in living her life by what she proclaims in her teaching, "You shall love the Lord your God with all your heart and with all your soul and with all your strength and with all your mind and your neighbor as yourself." Luke 10:27

Nancy McClintock with Bill, while Carl drove the tractor.

February, 1948, Frank celebrates his 68th birthday.

Frank and Martha's 50th wedding celebration with family and friends.

Gladys and Nancy Mae

Martha Patterson

Richard and Bill Taylor

Gladys Patterson Taylor and Dorothy Patterson

The Patterson Family with Nancy McClintock

The Patterson Family in 1955

The entire Covert Family with Frank and Martha

Frank at the Humble Mine

The Humble Mine

Slippery Rock, Pennsylvania